Lord, Teach Us to Pray

Alexander Whyte

BAKER BOOK HOUSE
Grand Rapids, Michigan

6884

Paperback edition issued 1976
by Baker Book House

ISBN: 0-8010-9511-5

PHOTOLITHOPRINTED BY CUSHING - MALLOY, INC.
ANN ARBOR, MICHIGAN, UNITED STATES OF AMERICA
1976

PREFACE

It is not the purpose of this Preface to anticipate the biography of Dr. Whyte, now being prepared by Dr. G. Freeland Barbour, or to provide a considered estimate of the great preacher's work as a whole. But it may be well briefly to explain the appearance of the present volume, and to take it, so far as it goes, as a mirror of the man. The desire has been expressed in various quarters that this sequence of sermons on prayer should appear by itself. Possibly it may be followed at a later date by a representative volume of discourses, taken from different points in Dr. Whyte's long ministry. It is a curious fact that he who was by general consent the greatest Scottish preacher of his day published during his lifetime no volume of Sunday morning sermons, though his successive series of character studies, given as evening lectures, were numerous and widely known.

At the close of the winter season, 1894-95, Dr. Whyte had brought to a conclusion a lengthy series of pulpit studies in the teaching of our Lord. It was evident that our Lord's teaching about prayer had greatly fascinated him : more than one sermon

upon that had been included. And in the winter
of 1895–96, he began a series of discourses in which
St. Luke xi. 1, " Lord, teach us to pray," was
combined with some other text, in order to exhibit
various aspects of the life of prayer. The most of
these discourses were preached in 1895–96, though
a few came in 1897 ; and at intervals till 1906 some
of them were re-delivered, or the sequence was
added to. On the whole, in Dr. Whyte's later
ministry, no theme was so familiar to his congregation or so beloved by himself as " Luke eleven
and one." To include the whole series here would
have made a volume far too bulky : in a sequence
stretching over so long a time and dealing with
themes so closely allied, there is a considerable
amount of repetition : it was necessary to select.
For instance, Paul's Prayers and Thanksgivings were
dealt with at length, and are here represented only
by two examples. Further, it has not been possible
to give the sermons in chronological order ; Dr.
Whyte dealt with the aspect of the matter upper-
most in his mind for the week, and followed no
plan which is now discernible : for the grouping,
therefore, as for the selection, the present editors
are responsible. They hope that the volume so
selected and arranged may be a sufficient indication
of the style and spirit of the whole sequence.[1] The

[1] The sermons on Jacob and the Man who knocked at midnight are parallel to the extent of a few sentences, and that on

Scottish pulpit owes much to " Courses " of sermons, in which some great theme could be deliberately treated, some vast tract of doctrine or experience adequately surveyed. This method of preaching may be out of fashion with the restless mind of to-day, but in days when it was patiently heard it had an immensely educative effect : it was a means at once of enlarging and deepening. And Dr. Whyte's people were often full of amazement at the endless force, freshness and fervour which he poured into this series, bringing out of " Luke eleven and one," as out of a treasury, things new and old.

Nobody else could have preached these sermons, —after much reading and re-reading of them that remains the most vivid impression : there can be few more strongly personal documents in the whole literature of the pulpit. Of course, his favourites appear—Dante and Pascal, Butler and Andrewes, Bunyan and Edwards : they contribute their gift of illustration or enforcement, and fade away. But these pages are Alexander Whyte : the glow and radiance of them came out of that flaming heart. Those who knew and loved him will welcome the autobiographic touches. In one of the

Elijah to the extent of a paragraph or two, with studies previously published in the *Bible Characters*. But they are so characteristic of the preacher, and so vital to the series that it has been deemed wise to give them, even though they are slightly reminiscent of matter which has before appeared.

sermons he recommends his hearers so to read the
New Testament that it shall be autobiographic
of themselves : if ever a man read his Bible so,
it was he. The 51st Psalm and many another
classical passage of devotion took on a new colour
and savour because, with the simplest and in-
tensest sincerity, he found his own autobiography
in them. Who that heard it spoken could ever
forget the description, given on one of the following
pages, of the wintry walk of one who thought himself forsaken of God, until the snows of Schiehallion
made him cry, " Wash me, and I shall be whiter
than snow," and brought back God's peace to his
heart ? But in a more general sense this whole
volume is autobiographic. " Deliver your own
message " was his counsel to his colleague, John
Kelman. He did so himself : it is here. One or
two ingredients in it are specially noteworthy.

1. One is his wonderful gift of *Imagination*. It
is characteristic of him that, in his treatment of his
chosen theme, he should give one whole discourse
to the use of the imagination in prayer. But there
is scarcely a sermon which does not at some point
illustrate the theme of that discourse. Here was a
soul " full of eyes." He had the gift of calling up
before himself that of which he spoke ; and, speaking with his eye on the object, as he loved to put it,
he made his hearers see it too with a vividness which
often startled them and occasionally amused them.

The Scripture scene was extended by some lifelike
touch which increased the sense of reality without
exceeding the bounds of probability. A case in
point is the man who knocked at midnight. "He
comes back; he knocks again : 'Friend!' he cries,
till the dogs bark at him." And sometimes the imagination clothes itself in a certain grim grotesquerie
which arrests the slumbering attention and is entirely unforgettable, as in the description of the
irreverent family at prayers,—their creaking chairs,
their yawns and coughs and sneezes, their babel
of talk unloosed before the *Amen* is well uttered.
These pages contain many instances of the imagination which soars, as he bids her do, on shining wing,
up past sun, moon and stars, but also of a more
pedestrian imagination, with shrewd eyes and a
grave smile, busy about the criticism of life and
the healthy castigation of human nature.

2. Along with this goes a strongly *dramatic*
instinct. This provides some words and phrases
in the following pages, which might not stand the
test of a cold or pedantic criticism. A strict editor-
ship might have cut them out : Dr. Whyte himself
might have done so, had he revised these pages for
the press. But they have been allowed to stand
because they now enshrine a memory : even after
twenty-five years or more, they will bring back
to some hearers the moments when the preacher's
eyes were lifted off his manuscript, when his hand

was suddenly flung out as though he tracked the
movements of an invisible presence, when his voice
expanded into a great cry that rang into every
corner of the church. In this mood the apostrophe
was instinctive : " O Paul, up in heaven, be
merciful in thy rapture ! Hast thou forgotten that
thou also was once a wretched man ? " Equally
instinctive to it is the tendency to visualise, behind
an incident or an instance, its scenery and back-
ground : " the man of all prayer is still on his
knees. . . . See ! the day breaks over his place of
prayer ! See ! the Kingdom of God begins to come
in on the earth." Occasionally—very ocasionally
but all the more effectively because so seldom—the
dramatic instinct found fuller scope in a lengthy
quotation from Shakespeare or even from Ibsen.
The intellectual and spiritual effect was almost
overwhelming the morning he preached on our
Lord's prayer in Gethsemane. Dwelling for a
moment on the seamless robe, with " the blood of
the garden, and of the pillar " upon it, he suddenly
broke off into the passage from *Julius Cæsar* :

> You all do know this mantle : I remember
> The first time Cæsar ever put it on.

It was a daring experiment—did ever any other
preacher link these two passages together ?—but
in Dr. Whyte's hands extraordinarily moving. The
sermon closed with a great shout, " Now let it

work!" and his hearers, as they came to the Communion Table that morning, must have been of one heart and mind in the prayer that in them the Cross of Christ should not be " made of none effect."

3. It was Dr. Whyte's own wish that he should be known as a specialist in the study of *sin*: he was willing to leave other distinctions to other men. No reader of these pages will be surprised to discover that, in the place of prayer which this preacher builds, the *Miserere* and the *De Profundis* are among the most haunting strains. The question has often been asked—Did Dr. Whyte paint the world and human nature too black? Even if he did, two things perhaps may be said. The first is that there are so few specialists now in this line of teaching, that we can afford occasionally to listen to one who made it his deliberate business. And the second is that the clouds which this prophet saw lying over the lives of other men were no blacker than those which he honestly believed to haunt his own soul. That sense of sin goes with him all the way and enters into every message. If he overhears Habakkuk praying about the Chaldeans, the Chaldeans turn immediately into a parable of the power which enslaves our sinful lives. Assyria, Babylonia, anything cruel, tyrannous, aggressive, is but a finger-post pointing to that inward and ultimate bondage out of which all other tyrannies

and wrongs take their rise. That is why a series of this kind, like Dr. Whyte's whole ministry, is so deepening. And that is also why these pages are haunted by a sense of the difficulty of the spiritual life, and especially of the life of prayer : we have such arrears to make up, such fetters to break ; we are so much encased in the horrible pit and the miry clay. The preacher is frank enough about himself : " daily self-denial is uphill work with me " ; and when in Teresa, or in Boston, or in the Puritans, he finds confession of dryness and deadness of soul, he knows that he is passing through the same experience as some of the noblest saints of God. If the souls of the saints have sometimes their soaring path and their shining wings, they at other times are more as Thomas Vaughan describes them, like moles that " lurk in blind entrenchments "—

Heaving the earth to take in air.

So these sermons become a tremendous rallying call to our moral energies, that we may overcome our handicap, and shake off our load of dust, and do our best with our exhilarating opportunity. Here the sermon on " The Costliness of Prayer " is typical : there is small chance of success in the spiritual life unless we are willing to take time and thought and trouble,—unless we are willing to sacrifice and crucify our listless, slothful, self-indulgent habits. This is a Stoicism, a small injection of which might put iron

into the blood of some types of Christianity ; Seneca
and Teresa, as they are brought into alliance here,
make very good company.

4. For the total and final effect of such preaching
is not depressing : it is full of stimulus and encouragement mainly because the vision of sin and
the vision of difficulty are never far removed from
the vision of *Grace*.   Dr. Whyte's preaching, stern
as the precipitous sides of a great mountain, was
also like a great mountain in this, that it had many
clefts and hollows, with sweet springs and healing
plants.   One of his most devoted elders wrote of him :
" No preacher has so often or so completely dashed
me to the ground as has Dr. Whyte ; but no man
has more immediately or more tenderly picked me
up and set me on my feet again."   Perhaps there
was no phrase more characteristic of him, either in
preaching or in prayer, than the prophet's cry, " Who
is a God like unto Thee ? "   And when at his bidding,
—with an imagination which is but faith under
another name,—we ourselves become the leper at
Christ's feet, or the prodigal returning home, or
Peter in the porch, or Lazarus in his grave, and find
in Christ the answer to all our personal need,—we
begin to feel how real the Grace of God, the God of
Grace, was to the preacher, and how real He may be
to us also.   This volume is full of the burdens of the
saints, the struggles of their souls, and the stains upon
their raiment.   But it is no accident that it ends

with the song of the final gladness : " Every one of
them at last appeareth before God in Zion."

When all is said, there is something here that
defies   analysis,—something   titanic,   something
colossal, which makes ordinary preaching seem to
lie a long way below such heights as gave the vision
in these words, such forces as shaped their appeal.
We are driven back on the mystery of a great soul,
dealt with in God's secret ways and given more
than the ordinary measure of endowment and
grace.   His hearers have often wondered at his
sustained intensity ; as Dr. Joseph Parker once
wrote of him : " many would have announced the
chaining of Satan for a thousand years with less
expenditure of vital force " than Dr. Whyte gave
to the mere announcing of a hymn.   That intensity
was itself the expression of a burning sincerity :
like his own Bunyan, he spoke what he " smartingly
did feel."   And, though his own hand would very
quickly have been raised to check any such testimony
while he was alive, it may be said, now that he is
gone, that he lived intensely what he so intensely
spoke.   In that majestic ministry, stretching over
so long a time, many would have said that the
personal example was even a greater thing than the
burning words,—and not least the personal example
in the matter of which this book treats,—the life
of prayer, ordered, methodical, deliberate, unwearied

in adoration, confession, intercession and thanksgiving. He at least was not in the condemnation, which he describes, of the ministers who attempt flights of prayer in public of which they know nothing in private. He had his reward in the fruitfulness of his pulpit work and in the glow he kindled in multitudes of other souls. He has it still more abundantly now in that glorified life of which even his soaring imagination could catch only an occasional rapturous glimpse. So we number him among those who through a long pilgrimage patiently pursued the Endless Quest, and who now have reached, beyond the splendours of the sunset, the one satisfying Goal.

CONTENTS

PART I

INTRODUCTORY AND GENERAL

CONTENTS

XIII. ONE OF PAUL'S THANKSGIVINGS . . 157

"Lord, teach us to pray."—LUKE xi. 1.
"Giving thanks unto the Father . . ."—COL. i.
12, 13.

XIV. THE MAN WHO KNOCKED AT MIDNIGHT . 169

"Lord, teach us to pray."—LUKE xi. 1.
"Which of you shall have a friend, and shall go
unto him at midnight . . ."—LUKE xi. 5–8.

PART III

SOME ASPECTS OF THE WAY OF PRAYER

XV. PRAYER TO THE MOST HIGH . . . 183

"Lord, teach us to pray."—LUKE xi. 1.
"They return, but not to the Most High."—HOS.
vii. 16.

XVI. THE COSTLINESS OF PRAYER . . . 194

"Lord, teach us to pray."—LUKE xi. 1.
"And ye shall seek Me, and find Me, when ye
shall search for Me with all your heart."—
JER. xxix. 13.

XVII. REVERENCE IN PRAYER 205

"Lord, teach us to pray."—LUKE xi. 1.
"Offer it now unto thy governor; will he be pleased
with thee, or accept thy person? saith the Lord
of hosts."—MAL. i. 8.

XVIII. THE PLEADING NOTE IN PRAYER . . 215

"Lord, teach us to pray."—LUKE xi. 1.
"Let us plead together."—ISA. xliii. 26.

PART I

INTRODUCTORY AND GENERAL

I

THE MAGNIFICENCE OF PRAYER

"Lord, teach us to pray."—LUKE xi. 1.
"A royal priesthood."—1 PET. ii. 9.

"I AM an apostle," said Paul, "I magnify mine office." And we also have an office. Our office is not the apostolic office, but Paul would be the first to say to us that our office is quite as magnificent as ever his office was. Let us, then, magnify our office. Let us magnify its magnificent opportunities; its momentous duties; and its incalculable and everlasting rewards. For our office is the "royal priesthood." And we do not nearly enough magnify and exalt our royal priesthood. To be "kings and priests unto God"—what a magnificent office is that! But then, we who hold that office are men of such small and such mean minds, our souls so decline and so cleave to this earth, that we never so much as attempt to rise to the height and the splendour of our magnificent office. If our minds were only enlarged and exalted at all up to our office, we would be found of God far oftener than we are, with our sceptre in our hand, and with our mitre upon our head. If we magnified our office, as Paul magnified

his office, we would achieve as magnificent results
in our office as ever he achieved in his. The truth
is,—Paul's magnificent results were achieved more
in our office than in his own. It was because Paul
added on the royal priesthood to the Gentile apostleship that he achieved such magnificent results in
that apostleship. And, if we would but magnify
our royal priesthood as Paul did—it hath not entered
into our hearts so much as to conceive what God
hath prepared for those who properly perform their
office, as Kings and Priests unto God.

Prayer is the magnificent office it is, because it is
an office of such a magnificent kind. Magnificence
is of many kinds, and magnificent things are more
or less magnificent according to their kind. This
great globe on which it strikes its roots and grows
is magnificent in size when compared with that
grain of mustard seed : but just because that grain
of mustard seed is a seed and grows, that smallest
of seeds is far greater than the great globe itself. A
bird on its summer branch is far greater than the
great sun in whose warmth he builds and sings,
because that bird has life and love and song, which
the sun, with all his immensity of size, and with all
his light and heat, has not. A cup of cold water
only, given to one of these little ones in the name
of a disciple, is a far greater offering before God
than thousands of rams, and ten thousands of rivers
of oil ; because there is charity in that cup of cold

water. And an ejaculation, a sigh, a sob, a tear, a smile, a psalm, is far greater to God than all the oblations, and incense, and new moons, and Sabbaths, and calling of assemblies, and solemn meetings of Jerusalem, because repentance and faith and love and trust are in that sob and in that psalm. And the magnificence of all true prayer—its nobility, its royalty, its absolute divinity—all stand in this, that it is the greatest kind of act and office that man, or angel, can ever enter on and perform. Earth is at its very best, and heaven is at its very highest, when men and angels magnify their office of prayer and of praise before the throne of God.

1. The magnificence of God is the source and the measure of the magnificence of prayer. " Think magnificently of God," said Paternus to his son. Now that counsel is the sum and substance of this whole matter. For the heaven and the earth ; the sun and the moon and the stars ; the whole opening universe of our day ; the Scriptures of truth, with all that they contain ; the Church of Christ, with all her services and all her saints—all are set before us to teach us and to compel us indeed to " think magnificently of God." And they have all fulfilled the office of their creation when they have all combined to make us think magnificently of their Maker. Consider the heavens, the work of His fingers, the moon and the stars, which He hath ordained : consider the intellectual heavens also, angels and

archangels, cherubim and seraphim : consider mankind also, made in the image of God : consider Jesus Christ, the express image of His person : consider a past eternity and a coming eternity, and the revelation thereof that is made to us in the Word of God, and in the hearts of His people—and I defy you to think otherwise than magnificently of God. And, then, after all that, I equally defy you to forget, or neglect, or restrain prayer. Once you begin to think aright of Him Who is the Hearer of prayer ; and Who waits, in all His magnificence, to be gracious to you—I absolutely defy you to live any longer the life you now live. " First of all, my child," said Paternus to his son, " think magnificently of God. Magnify His providence : adore His power : frequent His service ; and pray to Him frequently and instantly. Bear Him always in your mind : teach your thoughts to reverence Him in every place, for there is no place where He is not. Therefore, my child, fear and worship, and love God ; first, and last, think magnificently of God."

2. " Why has God established prayer ? " asks Pascal. And Pascal's first answer to his own great question is this. God has established prayer in the moral world in order " to communicate to His creatures the dignity of causality." That is to say, to give us a touch and a taste of what it is to be a Creator. But then, " there are some things ulti-

mate and incausable," says Bacon, that inter-
preter of nature. And whatever things are indeed
ultimate to us, and incausable by us, them God
" hath put in His own power." But there are many
other things, and things that far more concern us,
that He communicates to us to have a hand of
cause and creation in. Not immediately, and at
our own rash and hot hand, and at our precipitate
and importunate will, but always under His Holy
Hand, and under the tranquillity of His Holy Will.
We hold our office and dignity of causality and
creation under the Son, just as He holds His
again under the Father. But instead of that lessen-
ing our dignity, to us, it rather ennobles and endears
our dignity. All believers are agreed that they
would rather hold their righteousness of Christ
than of themselves ; and so would all praying men :
they would rather that all things had their spring
and rise and rule in the wisdom and the love and
the power of God, than in their own wisdom and
love and power, even if they had the wisdom and
the love and the power for such an office. But then,
again, just as all believing men put on Jesus Christ
to justification of life, so do they all put on, under
Him, their royal robe and their priestly diadem
and breastplate. And that, not as so many beautiful ornaments, beautiful as they are, but as instruments and engines of divine power. " Thus saith
the Lord, the Holy One of Israel,"—as He clothes

His priests with salvation,—" Ask Me of things to come concerning My sons, and concerning the work of My hands command ye Me." What a thing for God to say to man ! What a magnificent office ! What a more than royal dignity ! What a gracious command, and what a sure encouragement is that to pray ! For ourselves, first, as His sons,—if His prodigal and dishonourable sons,—and then for our fellows, even if they are as prodigal and as undeserving as we are. Ask of Me ! Even when a father is wounded and offended by his son, even then, you feel sure that you have his heartstrings in your hand when you go to ask him for things that concern his son ; and that even though he is a bad son : even when he sends you away in anger, his fatherly bowels move over you as you depart : and he looks out at his door to see if you are coming back to ask him again concerning his son. And when you take boldness and venture back, he falls on your neck and says, Command me all that is in your heart concerning my son. Now, that is the " dignity of causality," that in which you are the cause of a father taking home again his son : and the cause of a son saying, I will arise and go to my father. That is your " magnificent office." That is your " royal priesthood."

3. And, then, there is this magnificent and right noble thing in prayer. Oh, what a noble God we have !—says Pascal,—that God shares His

creatorship with us ! And I will, to the praise and
the glory of God this day, add this, that He makes us
the architects of our own estates, and the fashioners
of our own fortunes. It is good enough to have an
estate left us in this life, if we forget we have it :
it is good enough that we inherit a fortune in this
world's goods, if it is not our lasting loss. Only
there is nothing great, nothing noble, nothing
magnanimous or magnificent in that. But to have
begun life with nothing, and to have climbed up by
pure virtue, by labour, and by self-denial, and by
perseverance, to the very top,—this world has no
better praise to give her best sons than that. But
there is another, and a better world, of which this
world at its best is but the scaffolding, the preparation, and the porch : and to be the architect
of our own fortune in *that* world will be to our everlasting honour. Now, there is this magnificence
about the world of prayer, that in it we work out,
not our own bare and naked and " scarce " salvation only, but our everlasting inheritance, in-
corruptible and undefilable, with all its unsearchable riches. Heaven and earth, time and eternity,
creation and providence, grace and glory, are all
laid up in Christ ; and then Christ and all His
unsearchable riches are laid open to prayer ; and
then it is said to every one of us—Choose you all
what you will have, and command Me for it ! All
God's grace, and all His truth, has been coined—

as Goodwin has it—out of purposes into promises;
and then all those promises are made " Yea and
amen " in Christ ; and then out of Christ, they are
published abroad to all men in the word of the
Gospel ; and, then, all men who read and hear the
Gospel are put upon their mettle.   For what a
man loves, that that man is.   What a man chooses
out of a hundred offers, you are sure by that who
and what that man is.   And accordingly, put the
New Testament in any man's hand, and set the
Throne of Grace wide open before any man, and you
need no omniscience to tell you that man's true
value.   If he lets his Bible lie unopened and un-
read : if he lets God's Throne of Grace stand till
death, idle and unwanted : if the depth and the
height, the nobleness and the magnificence, the
goodness and the beauty of divine things have no
command over him, and no attraction to him—
then, you do not wish me to put words upon the
meanness of that man's mind.   Look yourselves
at what he has chosen : look and weep at what he
has neglected, and has for ever lost !   But there are
other men : there are men of a far nobler blood than
that man is : there are great men, royal men : there
are some men made of noble stuff, and cast into
a noble mould.   And you will never satisfy or
quiet those men with all you can promise them or
pour out upon them in this life.   They are men of a
magnificent heart, and only in prayer have their

hearts ever got full scope and a proper atmosphere. They would die if they did not pray. They magnify their office. You cannot please them better than to invite and ask them to go to their God in your behalf. They would go of their own motion and accord for you, even if you never asked them. They have prayed for you before you asked them, more than you know. They are like Jesus Christ in this; and He will acknowledge them in this. While you were yet their enemies, they prayed for you, and as good as died for you. And when you turn to be their enemies again, they will have their revenge on you at the mercy seat. When you feel, somehow, as if coals of fire were—from somewhere—being heaped upon your head, it is from the mercy seat, where that magnanimous man is retaliating upon you. Now not Paul himself ever magnified his office more or better than that. And it was in that very same way that our Lord magnified His royal priesthood when He had on His crown of thorns on the cross, and when His shame covered Him as a robe and a diadem in the sight of God, and when He interceded and said—" They know not what they do."

4. And then there is this fine and noble thing about prayer also, that the acceptableness of it, and the power of it, are in direct proportion to the secrecy and the spirituality of it. As its stealth is : as its silence is : as its hiddenness away with

God is : as its unsuspectedness and undeservedness
with men is : as its pure goodness, pure love, and
pure goodwill are—so does prayer perform its
magnificent part when it is alone with God. The
true closet of the true saint of God is not built of
stone and lime. The secret place of God, and His
people, is not a thing of wood and iron, and bolts
and bars. At the same time, Christ did say—*Shut
your door*. And in order to have the Holy Ghost all
to himself, and to be able to give himself up wholly
—body, soul and spirit—to the Holy Ghost, the
man after God's own heart in prayer always as a
matter of fact builds for himself a little sanctuary,
all his own ; not to shut God in, but to shut all that
is not of God out. He builds a house for God,
before he has as yet built a house for himself. You
would not believe it about that man of secret
prayer. When you see and hear him, he is the
poorest, the meekest, the most contrite, and the
most silent of men : and you rebuke him because
he so trembles at God's word. If you could but
see him when he is alone with the King ! If you
could but see his nearness and his boldness ! You
would think that he and the King's Son had been
born and brought up together—such intimacies,
and such pass-words, are exchanged between them.
You would wonder, you would not believe your
eyes and your ears. If you saw him on his knees
you would see a sight. Look ! He is in the

Audience Chamber. Look! He is in the Council
Chamber now. He has a seat set for him among
the peers. He is set down among the old nobility
of the Empire. The King will not put on His signet
ring to seal a command, till your friend has been
heard. " Command Me," the King says to him.
" Ask Me," He says, " for the things of My sons :
command Me things to come concerning them " !
And, as if that were not enough, that man of all-
prayer is still on his knees. He is " wrestling " on
his knees. There is no enemy there that I can
see. There is nothing and no one that I can see
near him : and yet he wrestles like a mighty man.
What is he doing with such a struggle ? Doing ?
Do you not know what he is doing ? He is moving
heaven and earth. The man is removing mountains. He is casting this mountain, and that, into
the midst of the sea. He is casting down thrones.
He is smiting old empires of time to pieces. Yes :
he is wrestling indeed ! For he is wrestling now
with God ; and now with man : now with death ;
and now with hell. See ! the day breaks over his
place of prayer ! See ! the Kingdom of God begins
to come in on the earth ! What a spot is that !
What plots are hatched there ! What conspiracies
are planned there ! How dreadful is this place !
Let us escape for our life out of it ! Is that man,
in there with God, your friend ? Can you trust
him with God ? Will he speak about you when he

is in audience ? And what will he say ? Has he
anything against you ? Have you anything on
your conscience, or in your heart, against him ?
Then I would not be you, for a world ! But no !
Hear him ! What is that he says ? I declare I
hear your name, and your children's names ! And
the King stretches forth His sceptre, and your
friend touches it. He has " commanded " his God
for you. He has " asked concerning " you and your
sons. Such access, such liberty, such power, such
prevalency, such a magnificent office has he, who
has been made of God a King and a Priest unto
God.

5. And, then, to cap and to crown it all—the
supreme magnanimity, and the superb generosity
of God, to its top perfection, is seen in this—in the
men He selects, prepares for Himself, calls, con-
secrates, and clothes with the mitre and with the
ephod, and with the breastplate. It is told in the
Old Testament to the blame of Jeroboam, that " he
made an house of high places, and made priests of
the lowest of the people, which were not of the
sons of Levi." But what is written and read in the
Levitical Law, to Jeroboam's blame, that very
same thing, and in these very same words, God's
saints are this Sabbath day singing in their thousands
to His praise before the throne of God and the
Lamb. For, ever since the day of Christ, it has
been the lowest of the people—those lowest, that

is, in other men's eyes, and in their own—it has
been the poor and the despised, and the meek, and
the hidden, and the down-trodden, and the silent,
who have had secret power and privilege with God,
and have prevailed. It was so, sometimes, even in
the Old Testament. The New Testament sometimes broke up through the Old ; and in nothing
more than in this in the men,—and in their mothers,
—who were made Kings and Priests unto God.
" The Lord maketh poor," sang Samuel's mother,
" and maketh rich : He bringeth low, and lifteth up.
He raiseth up the poor out of the dust, and lifteth
up the beggar from the dunghill, to set them among
princes, and to make them inherit the throne of
glory." And the mother of our great High Priest
Himself sang, as she sat over His manger—" He
hath regarded the low estate of His handmaiden. . . .
He hath filled the hungry with good things ; and
the rich hath He sent empty away." This, then,
is the very topmost glory, and the very supremest
praise of God—the men, from among men, that He
takes, and makes of them Kings and Priests unto
God. Let all such men magnify their office ; and
let them think and speak and sing magnificently of
their God !

II

THE GEOMETRY OF PRAYER

"Lord, teach us to pray."—LUKE xi. 1,
"The high and lofty One that inhabiteth eternity."—
Is. lvii. 15.

I HAVE had no little difficulty in finding a fit text,
and a fit title, for my present discourse. The
subject of my present discourse has been running in
my mind, and has been occupying and exercising
my heart, for many years ; or all my life indeed.
And even yet, I feel quite unable to put the truth
that is in my mind at all properly before you. My
subject this morning is what I may call, in one
word,—but a most inadequate and unsatisfactory
word,—the Geometry of Prayer. That is to say,
the directions and the distances, the dimensions
and the measurements that, of necessity, enter into
all the conceptions of our devotional life. " Man
never knows how anthropomorphic he is," says
Goethe. That is to say, we do not enough reflect
how much we measure everything by ourselves.
We do not enough reflect how much we measure
God Himself by ourselves. Nor can we help ourselves in that respect. If we are to measure God

at all, we must measure Him by ourselves. We
cannot do otherwise. We cannot escape ourselves,
even when we think and speak of God. We
cannot rise above ourselves. We cannot cease
to be ourselves. And thus it is, that when
we think or speak of God, if we are to think
and speak of Him at all, we must think and
speak of Him—as the schools say—"in terms of
ourselves."

Nor are we to take blame to ourselves on that
account. For that is our very nature. That is
how we have been made by our Maker. That is
the law of our creation, and we cannot set that law
aside ; far less can we rise above it. God Himself
speaks to us in the language of men, and not in the
language of the Godhead. In our reason, and in
our conscience, and in His Word, and in His Son,
God speaks to us in the language of men. He
anthropomorphises Himself to us, in order that we
may see and believe all that, concerning Himself,
which He intends us to receive and believe. And
we must go to Him in the same way in which He
comes to us. All our approaches to God, in prayer
and in praise, must be made in those forms of
thought and of speech, in those ideas and conceptions, that are possible to us as His creatures. All
the same, it is well for us to keep this warning well
in mind, that we never know how anthropomorphic we are, in all our approaches to Him Whom

no man can approach unto, Whom no man hath
seen nor can see.

The moral and spiritual world is essentially and
fundamentally different from the physical and
material world. The geographical and astronomical dimensions and distances of the material
world bear no manner of relation at all to the
dimensions and the distances—so to call them—
of the spiritual world. We speak of Roman miles
and of German miles and of English miles, we speak
of geographical or of nautical miles, when we take
our measurements of the material world. But
the distances and the directions of the moral and
spiritual world cannot be laid down and limited
in such miles as these. When Holy Scripture
speaks of the "highest heaven," it does not speak
mathematically and astronomically, but intellectu-
ally, morally and spiritually. The highest heaven
is not so called because it is away up above and
beyond all the stars that we see. It is called the
highest heaven, because it is immeasurably and
inconceivably above and beyond us in its blessedness and in its glory ; in its truth, in its love, in its
peace, and in its joy in God. And on the other
hand, the deepest hell, that the Bible so often
warns us against, is not some dark pit sunk away
down out of sight in the bowels of the earth. The
true bottomless pit is in every one of us. That
horrible pit, with its miry clay, is sunk away down

in the unsearchable depths of every evil heart.
And again, when it is told us in the Word of God
that the Son of God came down from heaven to
earth in order to redeem us to God with His own
blood, we are not to think of Him as having left
some glorious place far " beyond the bright blue
sky," as the children's hymn has it. Wherein
then did His humiliation consist ? " His humiliation consisted in His being born, and that in a low
condition, made under the law, undergoing the
miseries of this life, the wrath of God, and the cursed
death of the Cross." That was His descent from
heaven to earth ; and it was a descent of a kind,
and of a degree, that no measuring-line of man
can tell the depth of it, or the distress of it, or the
dreadful humiliation of it.

Now to expound and illustrate some outstanding
Scriptures on prayer,—in the light of this great
principle,—take, first, this fundamental Scripture—
" Our Father *which art in Heaven.*" Now Heaven,
here, is not the sky. It is not the heaven of sun
and moon and stars. Heaven here is the experienced and enjoyed presence of God,—wherever
that is. Heaven here is our Father's house,—
wherever that is. Heaven is high up above the
earth,—yes ; but let it be always remembered and
realised that it is high up, as Almighty God is high
up, in His Divine Nature, above mortal man in his
human nature. It is high up as goodness is high

up above evil and as perfect blessedness is high up
above the uttermost misery. As often as we kneel
down again, and begin to pray, we are to think of
ourselves as at a far greater distance from God
than we ought to be, and now desire to be. All
true prayer is a rising up and a drawing near to God :
not in space indeed ; not in measurable miles ; but
in mind, and in heart, and in spirit. " Oh for a
mountain to pray on ! " thou criest. " A mountain,
and a temple on the top of it ; high and exalted,
so that I might be nearer God, and that God might
hear me better ; for He dwelleth on high ! " Yes,
He dwelleth on high ; but all the time, He hath
respect to the humble. " Wouldst thou pray in
His temple ? " says Augustine; " then pray within
thyself ; for thou thyself art the true temple of the
living God."   And great authority on these matters
as Augustine is, a still greater Authority than he is
has said, " Believe Me, the hour cometh when ye
shall neither in this mountain, nor yet at Jerusalem,
worship the Father. The hour cometh and now is
when the true worshippers shall worship the Father
in spirit and in truth ; for the Father seeketh such
to worship Him. God is a spirit : and they that
worship Him must worship Him in spirit and in
truth." And further on in the same spiritual
Gospel, we read this : " These words spake Jesus,
and lifted up His eyes to heaven." The Son of God,
who was all the time in Heaven, came so truly

down among the sons of men, that He lifted up His
eyes when He prayed to His Father just as we ourselves do. Though He knew that the kingdom of
Heaven was within Him, and not in the skies above
Him, yet, like us, He lifted up His eyes when He
prayed. He was in all points made like unto His
brethren ; and in no point more so than in this
point of prayer. It is built deep into our nature,
as we are the creatures of Almighty God, that we
are to lift our eyes, and look up, when we pray.
And the Son of God took on our human nature,
and prayed as we pray, kneeling down and looking
up, falling down, and lifting up strong crying and
tears. So anthropomorphic did the Son of God
become, so truly was He made of a woman, and
made under the whole law and the whole practice
of prayer, as well as under every other law of devout
and reverential men.

And then, to take an illustration of all this from
the opposite pole of things : " And not many days
after, the younger son gathered all together, and
took his journey into *a far country*, and there wasted
his substance with riotous living." Every intelligent child, who is paying attention, knows that
the far country into which that prodigal son went,
was not far away from his home, as China and
India, Africa and America are far away from Edinburgh. He did not travel to that far country by
any caravan of camels, or by any ship with sails.

That far country was far from his father's house
not in miles, but in bad habits. The far country
was not so many hundreds of thousands of miles
away. Its great distance consisted in so many bad
secrets that he never could tell at home ; till they
had to be told, and paid for by his father, if his son
was not to be taken to prison. I myself have known
that spoiled and prodigal and now far-away son,
oftener than once. I have baptized him ; and I
have recommended the Kirk Session to admit him
to the Table. And I have written him, to Australia,
and to America, and have sent him books with his
name written upon them, and have never got an
answer. The last time I heard of him, he was
breaking stones for eighteen pence a day. That,
fathers and mothers, is the far country of our Lord's
parable.

Then again, take this for another illustration of
my morally geometrical and spiritually topographical argument. " Out of the *depths* have I
cried unto Thee, O Lord. Out of *the belly of hell*
cried I. Out of *an horrible pit*, out of the miry
clay." Now just what depths were these, do you
suppose ? Where were those depths dug ? And
how deep were they ? Were they like the dungeon
of Malchiah, the son of Hammelech, that was in
the court of the prison ? Oh no ! When Jeremiah
sank in that deep mire he was in a clean and a sweet
bed compared with that which every sinner digs

for himself in his own unclean heart and in his own
unclean life. The horrible pit and the miry clay
of the sinful Psalmist was dug with his own suicidal
hands, deep down in his God-forsaken heart. Oh,
take care in time ! You men who are still young !
Oh, be warned in time, and by those who can testify
to you, and can tell you about the wages of sin ;
for the wages of sin is both banishment from the
presence of God here, and it is the second death
itself hereafter.

Then again, " *Come* unto Me, all ye that labour
and are heavy laden." Now, just how do we come
to Christ ? We come in this way. Not on our
feet, but on our knees. " Not on our feet," says
Augustine, " but on our affections." When we are
burdened in our minds ; when we are oppressed
with manifold cares and sorrows ; when we are
ill-used, humiliated, despised, trampled upon ;
when we are weary of the world and of ourselves ;
and then, when, instead of rebelling and raging
and repining, we accept our lot as laid on us by
God, and according to His invitation take all our
burden to Christ in prayer,—that is the way to
come to Him. That is to say, we come from
pride to humility ; and from a heart tossed with
tempest to a harbour of rest and peace ; and from
rebellion to resignation ; and from a life of unbelief
to a life of faith and love. Come unto Me, says
Christ to us, for I have all that rest, and all that

peace in My own heart; and I will share it all
with you. We do not come to Him by changing
the land, or the city, or the neighbourhood, or the
house, in which we have hitherto lived. We come
to Him by changing our mind and our heart and
our whole disposition : or rather, by coming to Him
in prayer, and in holy obedience, He produces all
these changes in our hearts and in our lives. " Come
unto Me, all ye that labour and are heavy laden,
and I will give you rest. For I am meek and lowly
in heart ; and ye shall find rest unto your souls."

And it is in this same spiritual and emotional,
and not in any astronomical or topographical sense,
that the sorrowful prophets and psalmists cry
continually, " *Bow down* Thine ear, O Lord, and
hear me." When you are lying, quite prostrate,
on your sick-bed ; and when you can only whisper
your wants, and scarcely that ; then your doctor
and your nurse bow down their ear to hear your
whispered prayer. And so it is with your sick soul.
" Bow down Thine ear, O God," you sigh and
say. " Bow down Thine ear, and hear me ; for I
am brought very low. I am full of pain and sores :
I am full of sin and death." " No poor creature,"
you say, " was ever so fallen and so broken, and so
far beyond all help of man as I am." And you
continue to sigh and cry, night and day ; till at
last you burst out with this song, " I waited
patiently for the Lord, and He inclined unto me

and heard my cry. And He hath put a new song in my mouth, even praise unto our God : many shall see it, and fear, and shall trust in the Lord."

And it is in the same moral and spiritual, and neither local nor topographical sense, that it is so often said that God is nigh to such-and-such men, and is far off, and turned away, from such-and-such other men. As in the text : "Thus saith the high and lofty One that inhabiteth eternity, whose name is Holy; I dwell in the high and holy place, with him also that is of a contrite and humble spirit ; to revive the spirit of the humble, and to revive the heart of the contrite ones." And again in the 34th Psalm : "The Lord is nigh unto them that are of a broken heart, and saveth such as be of a contrite spirit." And St. Peter puts the same truth in this way : "Yea, all of you be clothed with humility ; for God resisteth the proud, and giveth grace to the humble."

And again, in the same moral and spiritual and not locomotive sense, David has this : "Who shall ascend into the hill of the Lord ? or who shall stand in His holy place ? He that hath clean hands and a pure heart : who hath not lifted up his soul unto vanity nor sworn deceitfully." And so on, all up and down the Word of God, the attitudes and the movements of the body, and the directions and the distances, the dimensions and the measure-ments of the material world, are all carried over

into the life of the soul and especially into the
devotional life of the soul. And when that is once
well understood, and always remembered and
realised, great light will fall on the Bible teaching,
and on the Bible precepts, about prayer. And our
own life of prayer will be immensely enriched and
refreshed : it will be filled with new interest, and
with new intelligence, in many ways ; as you will
soon experience, if you follow out and practise the
teaching that these great Scriptures have offered
you.

Now, my brethren, much and long as I have
thought on this subject, and with care and labour
as I have composed this discourse, I am keenly
sensible of how immature and unfinished my treatment of this great topic has been. And then,
such subjects can only be set before a specially
intelligent and a specially interested and a
specially devotional audience. I entirely believe
that I have such an audience, to a great extent,
and therefore, I hope that you will take away
with you these imperfect reasonings and illustra-
tions of mine this morning ; and will faith-
fully and thoughtfully and perseveringly apply
them to your own reading of the devotional parts
of Holy Scripture, as well as to your own public
and private exercises of prayer and praise. The
subject demands and deserves all my might and
all your might too—both as preacher and hearers ;

for it is our very life. It came to pass that as He Himself was praying in a certain place, lifting up His eyes and His hands to Heaven,—when He ceased, one of His disciples came to meet Him, and said to Him, " Lord, teach us to pray." Now, he who teaches us a true lesson in prayer, whether it is Christ Himself, or David, or Paul, or Luther, or Andrewes, or our mother, or our father, or our minister, or whosoever ; he who gives us a real and a true lesson both how to pray, and how to continue and increase in prayer,—he does us a service such that this life will only see the beginning of it ; the full benefit of his lesson will only be truly seen and fully acknowledged by us when we enter on the service of God in that City where they "serve Him day and night in His temple." For there we shall see His face ; and there His name shall be in our foreheads. Amen.

III

THE HEART OF MAN AND THE HEART OF GOD

"Lord, teach us to pray."—LUKE xi. 1.
"Trust in Him at all times; ye people, pour out your heart before Him: God is a refuge for us."—Ps. lxii. 8.

EVER since the days of St. Augustine, it has been a proverb that God has made the heart of man for Himself, and that the heart of man finds no true rest till it finds its rest in God. But long before the days of St. Augustine, the Psalmist had said the same thing in the text. The heart of man, the Psalmist had said, is such that it can pour itself out nowhere but before God. In His sovereignty, in His wisdom, and in His love, God has made the heart of man so that at its deepest—but for Himself—it is absolutely solitary and alone. So much so that,

> Not even the tenderest heart, and next our own,
> Knows half the reasons why we smile or sigh.

They see us smile, and they hear us sigh, but the reasons why we smile or why we sigh are fully known to God alone.

Now we all have hearts. Whatever else we have

or have not, we all have hearts ; and all our hearts
are of the same secret, solitary, undiscovered, un-
satisfied kind. And then, along with our hearts,
we all have God. Wherever in all the world there
is a human heart, God also is there. And He is
there in order to have that heart poured out before
Him. And out of that, out of the aloneness of the
human heart, and out of the nearness of God to
every human heart, there immediately arises this
supreme duty to every man who has a heart,—that
he shall at all times pour his heart out before God.
It is not the duty and privilege of psalmists and
great saints only. It is every man's duty, and
every man's privilege. And, indeed, all our duties
to God are already summed up in this one great
duty ; and all our privileges are held out to us at
once in this unspeakable privilege. " Trust in
Him at all times : ye people, pour out your heart
before Him : God is a refuge for us."

Now the whole profit of this fine text to us will
lie in our particular application of it to ourselves.
It is with this view that the text has been written.
The text rose, at first, out of David's experience,
and it is offered to us for our experience also. That
is the reason why those holy men of old wrote out,
to all the world, their most secret experiences.
They were moved to do so by the Holy Ghost in
order that we might learn to follow them in their
walk with God, and in their deepest spiritual life.

Come then, my brethren, and let us take lessons from those saints of God in their high and holy art. Let us go to their divine school, and learn of them how we also are to pour our hearts out before God. And let us take our first lesson from David in this fine psalm now open before us. When we really study the lesson he has set to us, we easily see how David came to be so tempted to bad passions and to evil thoughts of all kinds ; to revenge and retaliation against his enemies, and to doubt and despair of God's fatherly attention and care. As we also are often tempted in our adverse circumstances ; and that, in ways and at times that, like David, we can tell to no one. No man, we say with David, cares for our souls. But then, that is just our opportunity. That is just the very moment for which God has been working and waiting in our case. Do not let us miss it. Our immortal soul is in it. Our eternal life is in it. Only let us pour out all our loneliness and all our distress, and all our gloom, before God, as David did, and all will immediately be well. For either, He will remove our trouble at once and altogether ; or else, He will do better,—He will make His love and His peace so to fill our heart that we will break out with David and will sing : " In God is my salvation and my glory ; the rock of my strength, and my refuge is in God."

And, as with all our trouble, so let us do with all

our sins. For our sin is the mother of all our trouble :
get rid of the mother, and you will soon get rid of
her offspring. And the only way to get rid of sin—
as well as of sorrow—is to pour it out before God.
For one thing, you are often tormented and polluted,
—are you not ?—with sinful thoughts. Now as
soon as they enter, as soon as they arise,—pour
them out before God. Pour them out before they
are well in. Cleanse your heart of all unclean
thoughts, of all angry and revengeful thoughts ;
of all envious and jealous thoughts ; of all malicious
and murderous thoughts,—sweep them out as you
would be saved. Repudiate them. Deny them.
Denounce them. Declare before God, as He shall
judge you, that all these evil thoughts of yours
are not yours at all. Protest to Him that it is
some enemy of yours and His who always puts them,
somehow, into your heart. And pour them out like
poison. Pour them out like leprosy. For poison
and leprosy can but kill the body ; but bad thoughts,
entertained in the heart, will kill both body and
soul in hell. Let no sinful thought settle in your
heart for a moment. Call aloud on God the instant
you discover its presence. Wherever you are, and
however you are employed, and in whatever company,—that moment call on God. That moment
pour out your heart before Him. He knows all
that is in your heart in that moment of temptation ;
and He waits to see what you will say to Him

about your heart, and what you will do with it.
Disappoint Him not. Neglect Him not. Displease Him not. He has told you a thousand times
what you are to do at that moment. Do it. Do
what David did. Do what God's tempted and
tried people are doing every moment all around
about you. " Trust in Him at all times : ye people,
pour out your heart before Him : God is a refuge
for us."

" My sin is ever before me," says David in his
greatest psalm. And as often as his sin comes up
again before him, he makes another psalm concerning his sin and pours it out again before God. Do
the same. Do like David. His awful story is told
for your salvation. Speak then, to God, like David.
Say to God, like David, that that former sin of
yours is ever before you also. Say to Him that the
more you cleanse it away,—nay, the more He Himself cleanses it away,—the more somehow it is ever
before you. Say to Him that you cannot understand it, but that, the more you repent and turn
from your sin, the more you remember your own
evil ways, and your doings that were not good ;
and, the more you wash your hands in innocency,
the more you loathe yourself for your iniquities
and for your abominations. As often as such
terrible experiences as these visit you,—just remember poor sin-pursued David, and pour out all the
undying remorse of your heart again and again

before God. When your guilty conscience awakens
again on you, like the fury it is ; when you are not
able to look up for absolute shame ; even in the
hour of absolute despair ; even when death and
hell would almost be a hiding-place to you in your
agony,—fall down, and pour out all that before
God. For it is neither death nor hell that is a
refuge for you. Almighty God, and Almighty God
alone, is your refuge and the rock of your salvation,
and though you may have poured all that sin out
of your heart ten thousand times before,—pour it
all out again. And say to Him in your excuse
that your sin is ever before you. Ask Him to whom
you can go. Ask Him, tell Him, what is His name,
and what is His Son's name. And, as you pour
out your heart as never before, say as never before,—

> Rock of Ages, cleft for me,
> Let me hide myself in Thee!

" And a man shall be as an hiding-place from the
wind, and a covert from the tempest : as rivers of
water in a dry place, as the shadow of a great rock
in a weary land."

" At all times," is a most precious expression.
And as God would have it, for your instruction and
for mine, as to " times," I came the other day upon
these half-legible entries in an old black-letter Diary.
And indeed it was when I was spelling my way
through the rusty pages of that old diary that it
came into my head to preach this sermon. The

entries that specially bear on this text are these,—
I copy verbatim :

" *The fourth day of the week*—Wednesday. All
day, my heart has been full of wonder and praise
at God's extraordinary goodness to me. I went
back and back all day on the Lord's leading. Till
all day my heart has been one pool of love and
admiration as I poured it out before God."

" *The fifth day of the week*—Thursday," writes
this diarist, " is always a day of peculiar temptation
to me, and to-day has been no exception. I could
not go up into my bed till I had poured out all the
corruptions of my heart before God. And because
I could not sleep, I rose and went over the evil day
again, and made a more and more clean breast of it
all before God.

" *Die Dom.*" (a Latin contraction for the Lord's
Day). " Passed a poor day, but the clouds scattered
before sunset."

I was much struck with this, as I think you will
be. " *Communion Day*. For some time past I have
had to live in the same house, and even to eat at the
same table, with one I cannot bear with. I went on
sinning against him in my heart till the fast day.
When the Lord sent me a message by His servant
out of the 62nd Psalm "—our psalm, you see !—
" and I was able to lay His message to heart. On
the fast night I went to specially secret prayer and
poured out again and again and again my whole evil

heart before God.   Next morning I found it easy to
be civil and even benevolent to my neighbour.   And
I felt at the Lord's Table to-day as if I would yet
live to love that man.   I feel sure I will."   Yes,
ye people !   Pour out your heart in that way before
Him at all times, and on all the days of the week ;
God is a refuge for *us* also.

But with all that about God and about His people,
psalmists, and saints since then, the half has not
been told.   After all that, I have something still to
say that will add immensely to the wonder and the
praise of the text.   And it is this.   We do not,
properly speaking, pour out our hearts before God :
we pour our hearts *upon* God.   We do not pour out
our hearts before His feet : we pour out our hearts
upon His heart.   We do that with one another.
When we pour out a confession or a complaint or
a petition before any one we try to get at his heart.
We try to get at his ear indeed ; but it is really at
his heart that our aim is ; and much more so with
God.   We throw ourselves at His feet indeed ;
but, beyond His feet, we throw ourselves into His
bosom.   We press and pass through all His angels
round about Him.   We shut our eyes to all the
blinding glory.   We pass in through all His power,
and all His majesty, and all His other overwhelming
surroundings,—and we are not content till we come
to His heart, to God's very, very heart.   What a
thought !   Oh, all ye thinking men !   What a

thought! What a heart must God's heart be!
What knowledge it must have! What pity it
must hold! What compassion! What love!
How deep it must be! How wide! How tender!
What a mystery! What a universe we belong to!
What creatures we are! and what a Creator we
have! and what a God! "Oh, the depth of the
riches both of the wisdom and knowledge of God!
How unsearchable are His judgments, and His ways
past finding out! For of Him, and through Him,
and to Him are all things, to whom be glory for
ever. Amen."

And then, over and above all that, there is this
to crown it all. Not only do God's saints pour out
their hearts upon His heart: He pours out His
heart upon their hearts. His Son has come to us
straight out of His Father's heart. His Eternal
Son is ever in, and He is ever coming forth from,
the bosom of the Father. And then the Holy Ghost
comes into our hearts and brings God's heart with
Him. Which heart, it cannot be too often said,
He, the Holy Ghost, indeed is. That, O many
of my brethren, that is God's very heart, already
poured out this day upon your heart! That soften-
ing of heart under the Word, that strong, sweet,
tender, holy, heavenly spirit that has taken possession of your heart in this house. What is that?
What can it be, but God's very heart beginning to
drop its overflowing strength and sweetness into

your open and uplifted heart? Pour out your
thanks for that outpouring of His heart upon you.
And pour out your prayer for still more of His Holy
Spirit. Beseech Him not to take His Holy Spirit
away from you : say to Him that, in your estimation,
His loving-kindness is far, far better than life. Say
to Him that you have seen His power and His glory
this day, as His saints are wont to see Him in His
sanctuary ; and as He sees that you truly desire
it and truly enjoy it, He will say to you also :
" A new heart will I give you, and a new spirit will
I put within you. I will put My Spirit "—My own
Holy Spirit !—" within you, and cause you to walk
in my statutes, and ye shall keep My judgments
and do them."

I will not dwell on them, but I must mention
four reflections that have been much in my mind
all through this meditation.

First, the greatness, the all but Divine greatness
of the heart of man. I do not know that the highest
and most rewarded archangel of them all has an
honour and excellency of grace bestowed upon him
anything like this,—to be able to exchange hearts,
so to speak, with God : we pouring our heart upon
God, and He pouring His heart out upon us.

Second, the unspeakable happiness, even in this
life, of the man who pours out his heart, *at all times*,
upon God.

Third, the awful folly—were it nothing worse—

of carrying about a heart, and hiding a heart and all it contains, and never pouring it out upon God, even when permitted and commanded so to do.

And fourth, never for a day, never for an hour, forget this golden Scripture: "Trust in Him at all times: ye people, pour out your heart before Him: God is a refuge for us."

PART II

SOME BIBLE TYPES OF PRAYER

IV

JACOB—WRESTLING

"Lord, teach us to pray."—LUKE xi. 1.
"Jacob called the name of the place Peniel."—GEN. xxxii. 30.

ALL the time that Jacob was in Padan-aram we
search in vain for prayer, for praise, or for piety
of any kind in Jacob's life.   We read of his marriage,
and of his great prosperity, till the land could no
longer hold him.   But that is all.   It is not said in
so many words indeed that Jacob absolutely denied
and forsook the God of his fathers : it is not said
that he worshipped idols in Padan-aram : that is
not to be supposed—only, he wholly neglected,
avoided, and lived without God in that land.   In
the days of his youth, and when he was on his
fugitive way from his father's house, Jacob had
passed through an experience that promised to us
that Jacob, surely above all men, would ever after
be a man of prayer, and a man of praise, and a man
of a close walk with God, a man who would always
pay his vow wherever he went.   But Bethel—and
all that passed at Bethel—was clean forgotten in
Padan-aram ; where Jacob increased exceedingly,

and had much cattle, and camels, and maid-servants, and men-servants.

Time went on in this way till the Lord said unto Jacob: " Return unto the land of thy fathers and to thy kindred ; and I will be with thee." And Jacob rose up to go to Isaac his father in the land of Canaan. But every step that Jacob took brought him nearer to the land of Edom also : where Esau dwelt with all his armed men about him. And that brought back all Jacob's early days to his mind, as they had not been in his mind now for many years ; till, by the time Jacob arrived at the Jabbok, he was in absolute terror at the thought of Esau. But Jacob never lacked resource : and at the Jabbok he made a halt, and there he did this. He took of that which came to his hand a present for Esau his brother. For he said, " I will appease him with the present that goeth before me, and afterward I will see his face : peradventure he will accept of me." But, to Jacob's great terror, Esau never looked at Jacob's present, but put on his armour in silence, and came posting northwards at the head of four hundred Edomite men. Had Jacob had nothing but his staff with which he passed over Jordan, his mind would have been more at rest. But with all these women and children and cattle—was ever a man taken in such a cruel trap ? And he took them and sent them over the brook, and sent over all that he had. And when

the night fell, Jacob was left alone. Till every
plunge of the angry Jabbok, and every roar of the
midnight storm, made Jacob feel the smell of Esau's
hunting coat, and the blow of his heavy hand.
Whether in the body, or whether out of the body,
Jacob could never tell. It was Esau, and it was
not Esau. It was God Himself, and it was not
God. It was God *and* Esau—both together. Till
Jacob to the day of his death never could tell
who that terrible wrestler really was. But as the
morning broke, and as he departed, the wrestler
from heaven said to Jacob, " Thy name shall be
called no more Jacob, but Israel." And he
blessed him there. And Jacob called the name of
the place Peniel : which by interpretation is The
face of God : for he said, " I have seen God face to
face, and my life is preserved."

" Lord, teach us to pray," petitioned the disciple
in the text. Well, we see here how the whole of
Jacob's life was laid out, and overruled, and visited
of God in order to teach Jacob to pray, in order to
make Jacob a prince in prayer. And all his long
and astonishing story, with all its ups and downs,
is preserved and is told to us, to teach us also how
to pray. Lord, teach us to pray !

1. Well, the first lesson we are taught out of Jacob
is this—that as long as all goes well with us, we,
too, are tempted to neglect God : we seldom, or
never pray—to be called prayer. As Huysman

says in *En route*, " The rich, the healthy, the happy
seldom pray." You would have said that Jacob
had had such an upbringing and had fallen into
such transgressions, all followed by such mercies,
and by such manifestations of God, that he could
never again forget God. You would have said
that. But no sooner was Jacob safely out of Esau's
reach : no sooner had Jacob's affairs begun to
prosper in Padan-aram than Jacob's conscience
of sin fell asleep. And Jacob's conscience would
have slept on till the day of judgment had God and
Esau left Jacob alone. And that is our own case
exactly. " The heart is deceitful," says the prophet,
" who can know it ? " Well, we know it so far.
We know it thus far, at any rate—that we easily
forgive ourselves the hurt we have done to other
men. We have short memories for our own sins,
and for other men's sufferings. Only once in a long
while do we remember, and take to heart what we
have done to other men. We have a long memory
for what other men have done to us : but all that
is changed when we are the wrong-doers. Let those
who have suffered at our hands be long enough
out of our sight, and at a safe enough distance, and
we say, Soul, take thine ease. From the day of
the barter of the birthright, down to that arresting
night at the Jabbok, Jacob had seen himself, and
his share in all that bad business, with his own partial
and indulgent eyes. Whereas Esau had seen himself

with his own injured and angry eyes : and, for once, God had seen all that evil transaction with Esau's eyes also. Only, all the time that Jacob prospered in Padan-aram, God was as if He had not seen. God " winked," as we say, at Jacob's sin till Jacob was at the top of his prosperity, and then God opened His eyes on Jacob's sin, and He opened Jacob's eyes also. If you will read Jacob's Padan-aram life with attention—with your eye on the object—you will see that Jacob had no time in Padan-aram for prayer—to be called prayer. " Thus I was," complains Jacob, " in the day the drought consumed me, and the frost by night : and my sleep departed from mine eyes. Thus have I been twenty years." You know it yourselves, and you complain about it. What with the pressure of domestic duties : what with the tremendous and cruel competition of modern business life : what with the too late hours of the best society in the city : what with the sports and games of your holiday : and what with the multitude of books and papers of all kinds that you must keep up with—sleep even, not to speak of salvation, departs from your eyes. " Thus was I," complained graceless Jacob.

2. " So went the present over before Jacob : and himself lodged that night in the company." But Jacob could not sleep. He could not lie down even. He was in a thousand minds. He was tossed with tempest, and not comforted. And he rose up, and

sent over the brook all that he had. One thing
Jacob had quite determined on,—he would not return
to Padan-aram. At any risk, he would set his face
to go on to Canaan. And when he had taken the
decisive step of crossing the Jabbok, and when his
household had all laid them down to sleep—Jacob
was left alone, and Jacob set himself to " watch
and pray." Jacob, deliberately and of set purpose,
prepared himself for a whole night of prayer. " But
thou," said our Lord, " when thou prayest, enter
into thy closet, and shut thy door." Well, that
was just what Jacob did that night, and I suspect
Jacob, that he had not done so much as that for
the past twenty years. Leave me alone, he said.
Lie you down and sleep in safety, and I will take a
lantern and a sword, and I will watch the sleeping
camp myself to-night. And he did so. And that
is the second lesson out of Jacob at the Jabbok.
This lesson, namely : that there are seasons in our
lives when true prayer demands time, and place,
and preparation, and solitude. When we are full
of some great piece of business ; when a lawyer is
at a dying man's bedside taking down his last testament ; when a minister is in the depths of the
preparation of his sermon, and when the spirit of
God is resting on him with power ; when any really
serious business has hold of us, we have no scruple
in saying that we must be left alone. This, I say,
is the second lesson here.

Let a long journey then—by land or sea—at one time, be set apart for prayer. A whole day sometimes, a birthday, the anniversary of our engagement to be married, or of our marriage, or again an anniversary of some such matter as Jacob's deception of Esau, or of his flight, or what not. Every man's life is full of "days to be remembered." Then let them be remembered,—and with deliberation and resolution and determination; and your life will yet be as well worth writing, and as well worth reading as Jacob's life is. Insist that you are to be left alone sometimes in order that you may take a review of your past life, and at the same time a forecast of coming danger and death: and that will turn all the evil of your past life into positive good: that will take all the danger out of coming danger, and death itself out of fast approaching death. Make experiment: pray with deliberation, and with all proper preparation—and see !

3. Jacob, we are delighted to see, deliberately and resolutely set apart that whole night to prayer : and his prayer took him that whole night, and until the "breaking of the day." But, to do what ? Why did it take Jacob so long to offer his prayer ? Was God unwilling to hear Jacob ? No, that cannot be the true explanation. God was neither absent nor was He unwilling. God had come down to the Jabbok for this very purpose— to hear and to answer Jacob's prayer, and to pre-

serve Jacob's life from Esau's anger. God was
ready to hear and to answer : but Jacob was not
yet ready to ask aright. Jacob had twenty years
of unbelief and self-forgiveness, and forgetfulness
of Esau's injury, and total neglect and want of
practice in penitence, and humiliation, and sorrow
for sin. Jacob had all that, somehow or other,
to undo, and to get over, before his life could be
preserved : and the wonder to me is that Jacob
accomplished so much in such a short time. You
must all know how hard it is to put yourself into
your injured brother's place, and how long it takes
you to do it. It is very hard for you to see, and to
confess that God is no respecter of persons. It is
a terrible shock to you to be told—shall not the
Judge of all the earth do right between you and
your injured brother ? You know how hard, how
cruel, it is to see yourself as others see you, and
judge you : especially as those see you and judge
you who have been hurt by you. It is like death
and hell pulling your body and your soul to pieces
to take to heart all your sin against your neighbour,
as *he* takes it to *his* heart. And that is why Jacob
at the Jabbok has such a large place in your Bible :
because, what you have taken so many years to
do, Jacob did at the Jabbok in as many hours.
You surely all understand, and will not forget,
what exactly it was that Jacob did beside that
angry brook that night ? The evening sun set **on**

Jacob sophisticating, and plotting, and planning how he could soften and bribe back to silence, if not to brotherly love, his powerful enemy, Esau ; but before the morning sun rose on Peniel, Jacob was at God's feet—aye, and at Esau's feet also— a broken-hearted, absolutely surrendered, absolutely silent and submissive penitent. " In whose spirit there is no guile . . . I acknowledged my sin unto Thee, and mine iniquity have I not hid. . . . For this shall every one that is godly pray unto Thee in a time when Thou mayest be found : surely in the floods of great waters they shall not come nigh unto him."

4. But Jacob at the Jabbok always calls up our Lord in Gethsemane. Now, why did our Lord need to spend so much of that Passover night alone in prayer ? and in such an agony of prayer, even unto blood ? He did not have the sins of His youth coming back on Him in the garden : nor did He have twenty years of neglect of God, and man, to get over. No. It was not that. But it was this. I speak it not of commandment, but by permission. It may have been this. I believe it was this. *This*. Human nature, at its best, in this life, is still so far from God—even after it has been redeemed, and renewed, and sanctified, and put under the power of the Holy Ghost for a lifetime—that, to reduce it absolutely down to its very last submission, and its very last surrender, and its very last obedience,

the very Son of God, Himself, had to drag His
human heart to God's feet, with all His might, and
till His sweat was blood, with the awful agony of
it. " I have neglected Thee, O God, but I will
enter into my own heart," cries Lancelot Andrewes,
" I will come to Thee in the innermost marrow of
my soul." " It is true prayer, it is importunate,
persevering and agonising prayer that deciphers
the hypocrite," says Jonathan Edwards, repeating
Job. " My uncle," says Coleridge's nephew, " when
I was sitting by his bedside, very solemnly declared
to me his conviction on this subject. ' Prayer,' he
said, ' is the very highest energy of which the human
heart is capable ' : prayer, that is, with the total
concentration of all the faculties. And the great
mass of worldly men, and learned men, he pro-
nounced absolutely incapable of prayer. ' To
pray,' he said, ' to pray as God would have us
pray,—it is this that makes me to turn cold in
my soul. Believe me, to pray with all your heart,
and strength, that is the last, the greatest achievement of the Christian's warfare on this earth.
Lord, teach us to pray ! ' And with that he
burst into a flood of tears and besought me to pray
for him ! Oh, what a light was there ! "

5. We understand now, and we willingly accept,
and we will not forget Jacob's new name of
" Israel." Yes : it was meet and he was worthy.
For he behaved himself like a prince of the Kingdom

of Heaven that night. Prayer, my brethren, is princely work—prayer, that is, like Jacob's prayer at the Jabbok. Prayer, at its best, is the noblest, the sublimest, the most magnificent, and stupendous act that any creature of God can perform on earth or in heaven. Prayer is far too princely a life for most men. It is high, and they are low, and they cannot attain to it. True prayer is colossal work. There were giants in those days. Would *you* be one of this royal race? Would *you* stand in the lot of God's princeliest elect at the end of your days? And would you be numbered with His Son and with His choicest saints? Then, *pray*.

" Hitherto have ye asked nothing in My name: ask, and ye shall receive, that your joy may be full."

V

MOSES—MAKING HASTE

"Lord, teach us to pray."—LUKE xi. 1.
"And Moses made haste . . ."—Ex. xxxiv. 8.

THIS passage is by far the greatest passage in the whole of the Old Testament. This passage is the parent passage, so to speak, of all the greatest passages of the Old Testament. This passage now open before us, the text and the context, taken together, should never be printed but in letters of gold a finger deep. There is no other passage to be set beside this passage till we come to the opening passages of the New Testament. That day, on which the Lord descended, and proclaimed to Moses the Name of the Lord, that was a day to be remembered and celebrated above the best days of the Old Testament. The only other days to be named beside that day were the day on which the Lord God created man in His own image; and the day on which Jesus Christ was born; and the day He died on the Cross, and the third day after that when He rose from the dead. And then, the only days we have to set beside those great days are these: the day we were born, taken along with the

day we were born again ; and that best of all our
days, which we have still before us, that great day
when we shall awaken in His likeness. These are
the only days worthy to be named beside that great
day when the Lord put Moses in the cleft of the
rock, and covered him with His hand, and proclaimed, and said, " The Lord, the Lord God,
merciful and gracious " : and Moses made haste,
and said, " Take us for thine inheritance."

Now, what so draws us back to that Old Testament day, to that Old Testament mount, this New
Testament morning, is this : we find on that mount,
that day, an answer and an example to that disciple
who said, " Lord, teach us to pray." And that
answer, and that example, are set before us in these
three so impressive and so memorable words
" Moses made haste." And thus it is that if we
approach this text this morning in a devotional
mind, and in a sufficiently teachable temper, we
shall without doubt find lessons in it, and carry
away lessons from it—lessons and encouragements
and examples, and drawings to prayer and to
God, lessons and encouragements and drawings
that will abide with us, and influence us all our
days,—all our days,—till our praying days are done.

What was it, then, to begin with, that made Moses
in such a " haste " to bow his head, and to worship,
and to pray with such instancy at that moment ?
Well, three things I see, and there may very well

have been more that I do not see. But these three
things,—Moses' great need; God's great grace; and
then the very Presence of God beside Moses at that
moment. Moses was at the head of Israel. Moses
had everything to think of, and everything to do for
Israel. Israel was a child, and a wilful and a dis-
obedient child : and it all lay heavy upon Moses.
Moses had been put at the head of Israel by the
election and call of God. He had just led Israel out
of Egypt. The whole people lay beneath him at
that moment, spread out in their tents in the waste
wilderness. And Moses had climbed that mountain
that morning with a very heavy heart. It was but
yesterday that Moses had been so cut to the heart
with the awful fall of Aaron his brother—his awful
sin in the matter of the golden calf : and altogether
Moses was as near giving over and lying down
to die, as ever a despairing man was. It was all
that extremity and accumulation of cares and
labours and disappointments and despairs : and
then, at that moment, this so new, so unexpected,
and so magnificent manifestation of the presence,
and the grace, and the covenant-faithfulness of
God ; it was all that coming upon Moses at such a
moment, and in such a manner,—the stupendous
scene : the cleft rock : the Divine Hand : the
Divine Voice : the Divine Name : and Moses alone
with God amid it all,—it was all this that made
Moses make haste, and bow his head toward the

earth, and worship, and say, " Pardon our iniquity
and our sin, and take us for thine inheritance."

Archdeacon Paley discovered for us this feature
of Paul's mind and heart. Ever since Paley's day
it has been a proverb about Paul that he so often in
his Epistles " goes off on a word." Now what
word was it, I like to wonder, that made Moses " go
off " with such haste from listening to praying ?
All the words of the Lord moved Moses that day :
but some of those so new and so great words from
heaven that day would move Moses and hasten
him off,—some of them, no doubt, more than others.
Was it *I AM THAT I AM* : and then, *I will
cover thee with My hand while I pass by* ? Would
Moses need more ? What angel in heaven, what
saint on the earth would need more ? Or was it
I AM in His mercy ? or was it the same in His
grace ? or again in His long-suffering ? Whatever
it was, it had scarcely gone out of the mouth of God
when Moses had it in his mouth. Such haste did
Moses make, and so suddenly did his whole heart
go off and break out into prayer. The clear-eyed
author of the *Horae Paulinae* throws a flood of light
on the Apostle's mind and heart by pointing out
to us the New Testament words and New Testament things that made Paul so suddenly break off
into prayer and praise, into apostrophe and into
doxology. And it is delightful to watch and see
who " go off " into prayer and into praise : who at

one word of God, and who at another : who " make
haste," and because of what. We see some who get
no further than the very first word of the text.
Notably the 136th Psalm : " His mercy endureth
for ever." " His mercy endureth for ever." The
Psalmist's heart so hastens him in this matter that
he can only write a line at a time—when his hot
pen breaks in again with God's mercy. Six-and-
twenty times in one psalm does that Psalmist after
Moses' own heart " make haste " to hymn the
" mercy of God." The publican also in the Temple
" went off " on this attribute, till he was sent down
to his own house justified. " I obtained mercy,"
said the Apostle, " that in me first Jesus Christ
might show forth all long-suffering for a pattern."
" The Lord, the Lord God, merciful and gracious."

And Gracious! Not to speak of the countless
prayers, and psalms, and sermons that have taken
their stand on the Grace of God, we have a whole
masterpiece in our own tongue in celebration of
that Grace of God, and of that Grace alone. All
who have tasted what Grace is, either in religion or
in letters, must know and love that classical piece
which has *Grace Abounding* for its title-page.
" O ! to Grace how great a debtor ! " in that way
another in our own tongue " goes off " on the same
blessed word. " Long-suffering, forgiving iniquity,
trangression, and sin." How many have hasted and
bowed down at all these saving names of God !

And, how many fathers of children have " made haste " as they read that God sometimes " visits the iniquity of the fathers upon the children "! Now, as we know Paul so much better, when we know the words and the things that arrested him, took him captive, and started him off into prayer and praise,—so would we know and love and honour one another if we could be told at what name and at what attribute of God our neighbour makes haste to pray. They had a bold, childlike way in Israel with the names of God, and with their own names. At a child's birth they would take a Divine Name—El, or Jah, and they would add that name on to the former family name, and then give that compounded, fortified, ennobled and sanctified name to their child ; till that child, all his days, could never sign his name, or hear his name spoken, without his father's God coming up before him Now, which of God's names are so worked up and so woven into your home and into your heart ? Is it mercy ? Is it grace ? Is it long-suffering ? Or does God see you, as your son is born and so soon grows up, hastening lest it be said of you, " The fathers have eaten sour grapes, and the children's teeth are set on edge " ? What is it that makes you make haste like Moses ? If we knew, we should, in that, read your heart down to the very bottom. If we knew, we should know how to pray both for you and for yours as we ought.

But, once a man has begun to employ the promises of God in Holy Scripture in that way, Holy Scripture, and all its promises, will not suffice that man for his life of prayer. He will go on to make every book he reads a Scripture : and he will not long read any book that cannot be so made and so employed. Every book will become to him a word of God, and every place a mount of God ; and every new experience in his life, and every new circumstance in his life, a new occasion, and a new call to make haste to prayer. He will go about this world watching for occasions, and for calls, to prayer : he will be found ready and willing for all those occasions and calls when they come : and when they do not come fast enough, he will not wait for them any longer, but will himself make them. Every new beginner in prayer, for one thing, looks upon every approaching time and place of temptation as a summons to " make haste." And not neophytes and new beginners only; but the oldest saints, and the wariest saints and the least liable to temptation, will not think themselves safe without constant and instant prayer. Look at Christ. Consider the Captain of our Salvation Himself. Just look at the Intercessor Himself. By the time He came to His last trials and temptations—we should have thought that by that time He would have been above all temptation. We should have thought that by that time He would have fallen

back upon His Divine Nature : or, if not that, then
upon His perfect sanctification. But, what did He
do ? See what He did ! He cut short His great
sermon, after the Supper, in order that He might
get away from the upper room to the Garden to
pray. He made haste to get across the Kedron
to the place where He was wont to go alone at
night. He said, " Arise and make haste ; let us go
hence." And as soon as He was come to His closet,
among the vines and the aloes, He made haste to
shut His door till the blood came through His forehead, and fell down on the midnight grass. He
was in an agony, just as if He had been a new
beginner closing, for the first time, with the world
that lieth in the wicked one, and with the wicked
one himself. He foresaw the trials and the temptations of that night and that morning, and that
made him hasten away, even from the Lord's
Table, to secret prayer.

But not only when the Bible, with all its promises,
is in their hands ; and not only when trials and
temptations are at their doors, will your men of
prayer " make haste." Not only so : but if you
know how to watch their ways you will find something that is nothing short of positive genius in
their inventiveness, and in their manipulation of
these times and these places to make them times
and places of prayer. The very striking of the
clock—even in such a monotonous, meaningless,

familiar and commonplace thing as that, you will find some men every time the clock strikes, making haste again to pray. In curiosity, at this point, I rose from my desk and looked up two first-class dictionaries, and was disappointed not to find this sacred sense of the word, *Horology*, in either of them. But that did not matter. I know elsewhere the noblest sense of that neglected and incompleted word, independently of the dictionaries. And all the members of the classes [1] also know by this time the heavenly sense of Horology, though these dictionary-makers are ignorant of it. Yes, there have been men, and we know their names and have their " Horologies " in our hands—men of God, who have so " watched " unto prayer and have so numbered, not their days only, but their hours also—that their clock never struck without their making haste to speak again to Him, Who, in an hour when we think not, will say that time, with all its years and days and hours shall be no longer. They parted company with every past hour, and saw it going away to judgment with prayer : and they received and sanctified every new hour, consecrating its first moments to praise and prayer.

Then, again, the attractions of life, youth, manhood, middle life, declining life, old age : wise and prudent and foreseeing men take all these admoni-

---

[1] A reference to the St. George's Classes, which at that time 1895) were studying the Mystics under Dr. Whyte's leadership.

tions to heart and " make haste." Severe sickness
and approaching death make all men to be up
and doing. Donne, whom James the First per-
suaded to become a minister,—and to James, with
all his faults, we are deep in debt for that,—has left
behind him a very remarkable book, " Devotions
upon Emergent Occasions, and at the Several Steps
in my Sickness, Digested into Meditations upon our
Human Condition : into Expostulations and Debate-
ments with God : and into Prayers to Him, upon
the Several Occasions." Donne's all but fatal
illness came, according to his *Book of Devotions*,
through twenty-three stages : and at each new
stage the sick scholar, saint and superb preacher
made haste with another threefold Devotion. The
first, at the first Grudging, as the old doctors called
it, of his sickness : the third, when the patient
takes his bed : the fourth, when the physician is
sent for : the sixth, when the physician is afraid :
the eighth, when the king sends his own physician :
the fifteenth, when " I sleep not day nor night " :
the sixteenth, when I hear the bells ringing for
another man's funeral : the nineteenth, when the
physicians say that they see the shore : the twenty-
third, when they warn me of the fearful danger of
relapsing. " Most excellent Prince "—said Donne,
in dedicating his *Devotions* to James' eldest son—
" Most Excellent Prince, I have had three births—
one, natural, when I came into the world : one,

supernatural, when I entered into the ministry :
and now, a preternatural birth, in returning to life
after this sickness." And this is the best record,
and the best result to Donne, and to us of all his
births, and of all his health, and of all his disease :
this, that he was a man who " made haste " to
take all that befell him to God in prayer. " *Devotions*," he calls his work, " upon Emergent Occasions :
the Several Steps of my Sickness."

Others, again, will strike out ways of prayer and
a course of prayer in this way. One will take seven
friends, and, without telling them, he will make
himself certain to pray for them, by giving up a part
of each day of the week to each one of his seven
friends. And another will have seven children,
and he will distribute them over the week for special
and importunate prayer. Another will take certain
hours and certain days to work before God certain
vices out of his own heart, and life, and character,
and to work in, before God, certain virtues. Another
will have certain seasons, and at those seasons
certain devotions, to keep in mind some great catas-
trophe, or some great deliverance, or some great
and fearful answer to prayer, and so on. " Some
great calamity happens to you," says one of those
original men ; "you do very well to make it an
occasion of exercising a greater devotion."

But, excellent and approved and seen to be very
profitable as all that is, yet it is ejaculatory prayer

that is the perfection and the finish of all these
kinds of prayer in which we "make haste." And
when ejaculatory prayer has once taken possession
of any man's heart and habits, that man is not very
far off from his Father's house. For

> Each moment by ejaculated prayer,
> He takes possession of his mansion there.

Jaculum, all boys know, means "a dart." Ejaculatory prayer! A prayer shot up like a spear out
of a soldier's hand : shot up like an arrow sped off
an archer's sudden string! You have seen charts
of the air and of the ocean, with a multitude of
rapid and intricate lines to mark the origin and the
direction and the termination of the air and the
ocean currents. You have seen and have admired
beautiful charts and maps laid down like that.
Well, if you could, in this life, but be let see into the
Charthouse of Heaven, you would see still more
wonderful and still more beautiful things there.
You would see there, kept secret against the last
day, whole chambers full of nothing else, but of
charts and maps of ejaculatory prayer. You would
see prayer-plans of the cities and of the scattered
villages where God's best remembrancers are now
living,—plans and projections laid down and filled
up by those ministering spirits who are sent forth
to minister to them who shall be heirs of salvation.
You would see, filling the heavens above those cities
and villages, showers of ejaculatory prayer going

up and showers of immediate answers coming down. You would see shafts and darts and shootings upwards of sudden and short prayers wherever those men went in life, wherever they walked, wherever they worked, and wherever they went to rest and recreate themselves. From the street when those men pass along the street : from their tables where they eat their meals : from their beds : all day, and all night. You could follow and make out from these charts of ejaculation their times and their places of temptation. You would see a perfect sheaf of upward arrows, with all their points sharpened with love, as those men passed your house or met you in the street. Where you shot your arrows —not of prayer—*at them*, to your confusion you will see that they shot their arrows—not of envy or ill-will—*up to God*. What you see not now, you shall see hereafter. And that because, like all else in earth and in heaven, the chartularies of heaven and of earth will all be laid open at the last day : and then, when Christ shall appear, all who, with Moses, have " made haste " to pray shall appear with Christ in glory. And on that day, and at that hour, all those hidden schemes and methods and devices of secret and ejaculatory prayer shall be the astonishment of the whole world, and the admiration, and the praise, and the justification of God, and of all godly men, at that day.

"Seek ye the Lord," then, "while He may be

found, call ye upon Him while He is near." At every Name of His, call. Every time the clock strikes, call, ejaculate and call. For He saith, " I have heard thee in a time accepted, and in the day of salvation have I succoured thee : behold, now is the accepted time ; behold, now is the day of salvation." " To-day ; lest any of you be hardened through the deceitfulness of sin "

VI

ELIJAH—PASSIONATE IN PRAYER

" Lord, teach us to pray."—LUKE xi. 1.
" Elias . . . prayed in his prayer."—JAS. v. 17 (Marg.).

ELIJAH towers up like a mountain above all the
other prophets. There is a solitary grandeur about
Elijah that is all his own. There is an unearthli-
ness and a mysteriousness about Elijah that is all
his own. There is a volcanic suddenness—a volcanic
violence indeed—about almost all Elijah's movements, and about almost all Elijah's appearances.
" And Elijah the Tishbite, who was of the inhabitants of Gilead, said unto Ahab, As the Lord God
of Israel liveth, before whom I stand, there shall
not be dew nor rain these years, but according to
my word. . . . And the King of Samaria said unto
them, What manner of man was he which came
up to meet you, and told you these words ? And
they answered him, He was an hairy man, and
girt with a girdle of leather about his loins. And
the King said, It is Elijah the Tishbite."

And, then, this is the very last word of the very
last prophet of the Old Testament. " Behold,
saith the Lord, I will send you Elijah the prophet,

before the coming of the great and dreadful day of the Lord. And he shall turn the heart of the fathers to the children, and the heart of the children to their fathers, lest I come and smite the earth with a curse." And, then, in the opening of the New Testament, we hear our Lord speaking with great pride of the great austerity, the great solitariness, the great strength, and the great courage of Elijah. " What went ye out into the wilderness to see ? A reed shaken with the wind ? But what went ye out for to see ? A man clothed in soft raiment ? Behold, they that wear soft raiment are in kings' houses. But what went ye out for to see ? A prophet ? Yea, I say unto you, and more than a prophet. . . . And, if ye will receive it, this is Elias, which was for to come ! "

Elijah had a heavenly name : but he had, to begin with, an earthly nature. He was a man, to begin with, " subject to like passions as we are." Elijah was a man indeed of passions " all compact." We never see Elijah but he is in a passion, as we say. In a passion of anger at Ahab. In a passion of scorn and contempt at the priests of Baal. In a passion of fury and extermination against all idolatry, and against all organised uncleanness. In a passion of prayer and intercession. And, once —for, after all, Elijah is flesh and blood, and not stone and iron—once in a passion of despondency and melancholy under the juniper tree. Elijah was

a great man. There was a great mass of manhood
in Elijah. He was a mountain of a man, with
a whirlwind for a heart. Elijah did nothing by
halves. What he did, he did with all his heart.
And what a heart it was ! He, among us, who has
the most heart : he, among us, who has the most
manhood : he, among us, who has the most passion
in his heart—the most love and the most hate ; the
most anger and the most meekness ; the most
scorn, and the most contempt, and the most
humility, and the most honour ; the most fear, and
the most faith ; the most melancholy, and the most
sunny spirit ; the most agony of prayer, both in
his body and in his soul, and the most victorious
assurance that his prayer is already answered before
it is yet offered—that man is the likest of us all
to Elijah, and that man has Elijah's mantle fallen
upon him.

James, the brother of the Lord, and the author
of this Epistle, was nicknamed " Camel-knees " by
the early Church. James had been so slow of heart
to believe that his brother, Jesus, could possibly be
the Christ, that, after he was brought to believe,
he was never off his knees. And when they came
to coffin him, it was like coffining the knees of a
camel rather than the knees of a man, so hard, so
worn, so stiff were they with prayer, and so unlike
any other dead man's knees they had ever coffined.
The translators tell us that they have preserved

James's intense Hebrew idiom for us in the margin :
and I, for one, am much obliged to them for doing
that.   For, if I am saved at last, if I ever learn to
pray, if I ever come to put my passions into my
prayers,—I shall have to say to " Camel-knees,"
and to his excellent editors and translators, that I
am to all eternity in their debt.   The apostolic and
prophetic idiom in the margin takes hold of my
imagination.   It touches my heart.   It speaks to
my conscience.   And it must do all that to you
also.   For, even after we have, in a way, prayed,
off and on, for many years, in the pulpit, at the
family altar, and on the platform in the prayer-
meeting,—how seldom, if ever, we " pray in our
prayers " !   We repeat choice passages of Scripture.
We recite, with sonorous voices, most excellent
evangelical extracts from Isaiah and Ezekiel.   We
declaim our petitions in a way that would do credit
to a stage surrounded with spectators.   We praise
one man, and we blame another man, in our prayers.
We have an eye, now to this man present, and now
to that man absent.   We pronounce appreciations,
and we pass judgments in our prayers.   We flatter
the great, and we fall down before Kings.   We tell
our people what the Queen said to us, and what
we said to her.   We argue, and we debate, and we
reason together, sometimes with men, and sometimes with God.   " Come, now, and let us reason
together, saith the Lord."   Are you old enough to

remember Dr. Candlish's forenoon prayer? We used to say that his first prayer was enough for the whole of that day. He so " prayed in that prayer." He so came and reasoned together with God in that prayer. Sometimes he would take us to our knees till we had knees in those days like James the Just, as he led us through the whole of Paul's reasoning with God and with man in the Epistle to the Romans. Sometimes he would argue like Job, and would not be put down; and then he would weep like Jeremiah and dance and sing like Isaiah. That great preacher was an Elijah both in his passions and in his prayers. He would put all his passions at one time into an Assembly speech as he stood before Ahab, and at another time into a great sermon to his incomparably privileged people : but I liked his passions best in his half-hour prayer on a Sabbath morning; he so " prayed in that prayer."

You have not Elijah's prophetical office, not James's apostolical inspiration, not Dr. Candlish's oratorical power : but you have plenty of passion if you would but make the right use of it. You are all vicious or virtuous men, prayerful or prayerless men ; and, then, you are effectual or unavailing men in your prayers—just as your passions are. You have all quite sufficient variety and amount of passion to make you mighty men with God and with men, if only your passions found their proper vent

in your prayers. You have all passion enough—
far too much—in other things. What an ocean of
all kinds of passion your heart is ! What depths
of self-love are in your heart ! And what a master-
passion is your self-love ! Like Aaron's serpent,
your passion of self-love swallows all the rest of the
serpents, of which your heart is full. What hate,
again, you have in your heart, at the persons and
the things you do so hate ! What hope also for the
things you so passionately hope for ! Oh, if only
you had that passionate hope in your heart, which
maketh not ashamed ! " Yea, what clearing of
yourselves " there is in your hearts ! " Yea, what
indignation ! Yea, what fear ! Yea, what vehement desire ! Yea, what zeal ! Yea, what revenge !" Yes : you have passions enough to make
you a saint in heaven, or a devil in hell : and
they are every day making you either the one
or the other. We have all plenty of passion, and
to spare : only, it is all missing the mark. It is all
sound and fury, a tale told, a life laid out and lived,
by an idiot. Our passions, all given us for our
blessedness, are all making us and other people
miserable. Our passions, and their proper objects,
were all committed to us of God to satisfy, and to
delight, and to regale, and to glorify us. But we
have taken our passions and have made them the
instruments and the occasions of our self-de-
struction. We are self-blinded, and self-besotted

men : and it is the prostitution of our passions that has done it. Does the thought of God ever make your heart swell and beat with holy passion ? Does the Name of Jesus Christ ever make you sing in the night ? Do His words hide in your heart like the words of your bridegroom ? Do you tremble to offend Him ? Do you number the days till you are to be for ever with Him ? And so on— through all your passions of all kinds in your heart ? No, oh no ! Your daily life among these men and women is full of passion : but your heart in your religion is as dead as a stone. And you are not alone to blame for that. Your father and your mother, your tutor and your governor, taught you many branches of learning and perfected you in many accomplishments, as they are called : but they could not teach you to keep *this* passion in your heart, for they did not know the way. You never heard them say so much as the word " passion " in connection with prayer. And your ministers have not mended matters. They did not study the passions at college : at least, never in this light. They graduated in mental philosophy ; but it was falsely so called. Their first-class honours puffed them up : but they edified them not. And ever since, their own passions are all in disorder and death, and how then could they correct or instruct you ? Their own passions are not aflame within them with God, and with their Saviour Jesus

Christ, and with His Cross, and with His throne of judgment, and with heaven, and with hell.

The Bible, naturally, shows a preference for men of " like passions " with itself. The more passionateness any man puts into his prayer, the more space and the more praise the Bible gives to that man. Jacob will come at once to every mind. Now, why does Jacob come to all our minds at this moment ? Simply because he was a prince in the passionateness of his great prayer at the Jabbok. What a tempest of passion broke upon the throne of God all that night ! What a storm of fear and of despair, and of remorse, and of self-accusation, and of recollection, and of imagination, and of all that was within Jacob ! Jacob's passions literally tore him to pieces that terrible night. His thigh-bones were twisted, and torn out of their sockets : his strongest sinews snapped under the strain like so many silk threads. There was not another night like that for passion in prayer for two thousand years. Esau also often " halted upon his thigh " : but that was with hunting too hard ; that was with running down venison, and leaping hedges and ditches after his quarry. Esau wrestled with wild beasts. But Jacob,—he wrestled with the angel. And take Hannah as an example to wives and mothers. What a passionate, heart-broken, half-insane woman was Hannah ! For, how she " prayed in her prayers " ! She was absolutely drunk with her

sorrowful passion. She would have fallen on the
floor of the sanctuary as she reeled in her passion
had she not caught hold of the horns of the altar.
And Isaiah,—" Oh, that Thou wouldest rend the
heavens,"—and he rent them as he prayed: " that
Thou wouldest come down, that the mountains
might flow down at Thy presence. . . . But we are
all as an unclean thing, and all our righteousnesses
are as filthy rags ; and we all do fade as a leaf;
and our iniquities, like the wind, have taken us
away "—and a thousand such passionate passages,
both in preaching and in prayer. What a passion
for holiness had that great Old Testament orator !
And Ezra, who is too little known. " At the
evening sacrifice I arose up from my heaviness;
and having rent my garment and my mantle, I fell
upon my knees, and spread out my hands unto the
Lord my God, and said, O my God, I am ashamed
and blush to lift up my face to Thee, my God :
for our iniquities are increased over our head, and
our trespass is grown up unto the heavens. . . .
Now when Ezra had prayed, and when he had con-
fessed, weeping and casting himself down before the
house of God, there assembled unto him out of
Israel a very great congregation of men and women
and children: for the people wept very sore."
There also is passion in prayer for you ; and men,
and women, and children, all joining in it !

But time would fail me to tell all the passionate

prayers of the prophets, and the Psalmist, and the friend at midnight, and the importunate widow, and all ending in the Garden of Gethsemane. No : not all ending there—alas, alas ! would God that they did,—for our Lord passionately foretells certain passionate scenes that we shall all see, if we do not take a passionate part in them. " For, when once the Master of the house is risen up, and hath shut to the door, and ye begin to stand without . . saying Lord, Lord, open unto us ! there shall be weeping and gnashing of teeth, when ye shall see Abraham, and Isaac, and Jacob, and all the prophets, in the Kingdom of God, and you yourselves cast out." There is passion in *that* prayer, and in *this* : " Fall on us, and hide us from the face of Him that sitteth on the throne, and from the wrath of the Lamb ! "

And, now to sum it all up, and to lay it all to heart. Let every man here, henceforth " pray in his prayers " like Elijah and like James. That is to say, let every man put his passion into his prayers. And, then, what will take place in every man and in every man's house who lays up in his heart, and practises in his life, the lesson of this great Scripture ? This will take place in every such man, and in every such man's household. His heart will, by degrees, be drawn off the things of this deceitful and sinful world : and it will be directed in upon the great world within him, the

great world before him, and the great world above
him. The heat of his heart will all begin to burn
after heavenly things. And the man will, gradually,
as he continues to pray, become a new man, a new
son, a new lover, a new husband, a new father. His
passions that made him so impossible to live with
will all become subdued, and softened, and sweetened,
till he will be like a little child in your hands. He
was at one time so hard, and so harsh, and so
impossible to please, and so full of his own ideas
and opinions and prejudices and passions, so loud
and so wilful : but you never hear him now ; he
thinks you so much better than himself; he so
despises himself and so respects and honours
you. Patience and meekness and silence, and his
daily cross, are now the only passions of his heart.
Perhaps all that is taking place and going on in
your own house, and you do not see it or aright
understand it. James did not see nor understand
Jesus till Jesus was glorified. But it has been
prayer that has been doing it. Nothing does all
that in any house but prayer. Nothing silences,
and subdues, and sanctifies our passions but prayer.
His Prayer when you were asleep ! *His* Prayer
with passion, that had to wait for its full utterance
and for its full agony till you were fast asleep !
His Prayer also when you were neglecting Him,
and trampling upon Him !

Oh, I think you should cheer on and encourage

your minister to preach more about prayer ! And
about the place of the passions in prayer ! You
should buy the best books about prayer ! You
know their names, surely. You should send presents
of the best books about prayer ! It would soon
repay you ! It would soon be returned—into no
bosom so soon as into yours !—if you had even one
in your whole household who " prayed in his
prayers."

VII

JOB—GROPING

"Lord, teach us to pray."—LUKE xi. 1.
"Oh that I knew where I might find Him! that I might come even to His seat."—JOB xxiii. 3.

THE Book of Job is a most marvellous composition. Who composed it, when it was composed, or where —nobody knows. Dante has told us that the composition of the *Divine Comedy* had made him lean for many a year. And the author of the Book of Job must have been Dante's fellow both in labour and in sorrow and in sin, and in all else that always goes to the conception, and the composition, and the comprehension of such immortal works as the Book of Job and the *Divina Commedia*.

The worst of it was that Job could not find out, with all he could do, *why it was* that God had so forsaken him. Job had a good and honest heart, and a conscience void of offence both toward God and toward man. With the whole of the Book of Job in our hands, we know what neither Job, nor Eliphaz, nor Bildad, nor Zophar, nor Elihu knew. We have the key of the whole mystery, and the clue of the whole labyrinth, in our hands all the

time we read. We see the end from the beginning.
We see that Job, in all his terrible trials, was being
made a spectacle unto the world, and unto angels,
and unto men : a splendid spectacle as it turned
out, of patience, and endurance, and humility, and
resignation, and faith, and love. But what Job
knew not then he knows now, as he stands on the
sea of glass, having a harp of God in his hand.
"And they sing the song of Moses, the servant of
God, and the song of the Lamb, saying, Great and
marvellous are Thy works, Lord God Almighty ;
just and true are Thy ways, Thou King of Saints."

The captivity of Job arose out of God's pure and
unchallengeable sovereignty, as we say. God
deserted and forsook Job for reasons that were
sufficient to Himself, and in which He had no
counsellor. It was to silence the scoffs and sneers
of Satan : it was to produce a shining example of
submission and resignation, and trust in God, that
would stand out to the end of time : and it was to
perfect all these, and many other graces, in the
great patriarch himself that Job was so forsaken
of God, and had his faith and his trust in God put
to such a terrible test. That was Job's case. But
if we are in any such darkness to-day, the likelihood
is that our case is not such a mystery : our case is
not so deep and unfathomable to us as Job's case
was to him. To take a too common case. One
here will have lost God, just by " neglecting " Him.

In his inward relations with the soul, God, so to speak, does not thrust Himself upon the soul. He—so we must speak of such things—He sometimes stands aside, and apart, while persons and things take that possession of the soul which rightly belongs to Him. And, then, after a time, the silly soul comes to itself, and wakens up to see and to feel its bitter loss. "I have neglected Thee," cries out one who has taught many of us how to keep up a close walk with God. "God," says John Donne also, in a great sermon on the same subject, "God is like us in this also, that He takes it worse to be slighted, to be neglected, to be left out, than to be actually injured. Our inconsideration, our not thinking of God in our actions, offends Him more than our sins." "Pardon," cries Bishop Wilson, in his *Sacra Privata*, "pardon, that I have passed so many days without acknowledging and confessing Thy wonderful goodness to the most unworthy of Thy servants. Preserve in my soul, O God, such a constant and clear sense of my obligations to Thee, that upon every new receipt of Thy favour I may immediately turn my eyes to Him from whom cometh my salvation." Another in his evening prayer in his family says this: "We have fled from Thee seeking us: we have neglected Thee loving us: we have stopped our ears to Thee speaking to us: we have forgotten Thee doing good to us: we have despised Thee correcting us." Thus con-

fess before God Andrewes and Donne and Wilson.
Only,—these are quite exceptional men. And their
God has a sensitiveness, and a sensibility, so to call
it, toward such men,—a sensitiveness and a tenderness that He cannot have toward the common run
of His people. God comes far nearer to some men
than to others : and, then, on their neglect of Him,
He goes much farther away from them, and stays
away much longer. God's dealings with the com-
monalty of His people are much more commonplace, conventional, and uneventful than they are
with His electest and choicest saints. His relations
with them are exquisitely intimate, tender, easily
offended, and easily injured. But an example, and
an illustration from real life, and that too, among
ourselves, will be far more to the purpose than the
name of any great saint of other days, and far
more worth than any amount of generalisation and
description. Conversing the other day with one
of my own people, about the life of God in the soul,
he took me aside, and told me this. I have his
permission to tell it to anyone to whom it may be a
blessing to hear it. It was last summer, when our
congregation was scattered about, up and down the
country, and when some of the home restraints were
sitting somewhat loose on some of our people. The
first three weeks of his holiday—he gave me the
exact names and dates—he never had such a close
walk with God during all the thirty years—off and

on—that he has known God. But he had an invitation to spend ten days with one of ourselves : and
he set out, so he told me, to keep his engagement,
with some misgivings of heart that the visit would
be too much for him. But, as it happened, it turned
out far worse for him than anything he had antici-
pated. Such was the company of which the house
was full ; such were the conversations that were
permitted, and encouraged ; such were the books
that were read, and that were never read ; such
was the eating and the drinking; and such was the
keeping of the Sabbath, that, what with one thing
and what with another, he told me that he had read
little else but the penitential Psalms and the Book
of Job ever since, so exactly does that Book describe
his desolate estate to-day. Now, whether it was
his too great complaisancy with the secular-minded
company ; or, whether it was the part he took, or
did not take in the conversations; or whether it
was the talk about their absent friends, and the
fault-finding, and the detraction, of which that
house is notoriously full ; or whether it was that he
had come away and left at home his books and
papers, his habits in secret that so help him to keep
up his communion with God ; or whether it was his
miskeeping of the two Sabbaths that he was there,—
he did not particularise to tell me : and his soul
was too much in hell already for me to ask. Only,
he came and he went ; and no one in that crowded

house knew any more what was passing in that man's
soul, than Job's four friends knew the secret of the
Lord with His chastened servant. In ways like
these—in ways that nobody would believe—men
among ourselves also are crying to God night and
day in agony : " Oh that I knew where I might find
Him ! That I might come even to His seat ! "

Now, when we set out to seek for anything that
we have lost, we do not go gaping about anywhere
and everywhere. We go straight to the place where
we lost it. We retrace our steps to the exact spot
where we wakened up to miss the thing we now
value and miss so much. Go back, then, to that sad
house where God, in His anger at you, forsook you.
On what day ? at what hour ? On what occasion
was it ? Was it when you were sitting at table, and
forgetting yourself ? Was it during that ever-to-be-
lamented and never-to-be-recalled conversation ?
Was it at that moment when the golden rule leapt
too late into your mind ? You would not have
believed it beforehand that Almighty God would
have descended to take notice of such trifles. That
He would have taken a passing indiscretion in eating, and drinking, and conversation, so much to
heart ! and would have kept it up so long against
you,—you would not have believed it, if you had
not yourself experienced it. No ! But He has
taken you this time out of all men's hands into His
own hands. And, on your own admission, He is

teaching you a lesson, this time, that you will not soon forget. He will teach you that there is nothing He takes so mighty ill at your hand as just the way you transgress against your brother, and let other men transgress against him, when you are his only friend. A new commandment,—He has said to you at a hundred communion tables,—that you do to others as you would they did to you. But God does not cast off for ever: all God's people will testify and tell you. No. But you will have to seek Him with many bitter complaints against yourself this time, and with very determined intentions and resolutions for the time to come.

Would you know, then, where you may have any hope to find Him? Would you come this day to His seat? Would you have it again, between Him and you, as it was in months past, and as it was in the days when God preserved you? Well,—come this way. Try this door. I do not say that you will find Him at your first approach and prayer. You may, or you may not. God is not mocked God is not to be set aside, and His holy law, just when it suits you and your company. But that being admitted, try this. Deny yourself. " Mortify your members, which are on the earth." Take up your cross daily in that thing concerning which God has had a controversy with you in your conscience secretly ever since. Was it in eating or drinking? Was it in bad temper? Was it in envy and ill-will?

Was it in that sweet conversation in which you sat and spoke such unanimous things to the depreciation and damage of your brother ? If it was, try this. I have known this work well. I have known it work an immediate miracle. Go straight to your brother to-day : or take pen and ink, and tell him that you have not had a dog's life with God ever since. " When I kept silence, my bones waxed old through my roaring all the day long. For day and night Thy hand was heavy upon me : my moisture is turned into the drought of summer. I acknowledged my sin unto Thee, and mine iniquity have I not hid. I said, I will confess my transgressions unto the Lord : and Thou forgavest the iniquity of my sin."

Is it "even to His seat," then, that you would fain come ? Is your cause ready to be "ordered before Him " ? And is your mouth "filled with arguments," if you could only come to His seat ? Well, know you not where His seat really and truly is ? What ! Know you not that His seat is within you,—even within your heart ? " When I was a child, I spake as a child, I understood as a child, I thought as a child." It was when Israel was a child that God came down, and sat upon a mercy-seat of pure gold : two cubits and a half was the length of it, and a cubit and a half the breadth of it, with the cherubim stretching forth their wings on high. It was when Israel was still a child that

he went up, now to this mountain of Samaria and
now to that mountain of Jerusalem, saying, as he
went up : " Oh that I knew where I might find
Him ! That I might come even to His seat ! "
But, finding fault with those childish days, God has
now said, " Know ye not that *ye* are the temple
of God, and that the spirit of God dwelleth in *you* ?
Know ye not that *your body* is the temple of the
Holy Ghost which is in you, and which ye have of
God ? "   And again,—for ever since the fulness of
time our New Testament is full of it,—" Say not in
thine heart, Who shall ascend into heaven ? (that
is, to bring Christ down from above :) or, Who shall
descend into the deep? (that is, to bring up Christ
again from the dead.)   But what saith it ?   The
word is nigh thee, even in thy mouth, and in thy
heart."

At the same time, it is the last thing we are able
and willing to do,—to cease to be children, and to
grow up to be men, in the things of God. To learn
and know that God is a spirit, and that He dwells
not in temples made with hands ; but that His
true and only temple is the temple of the penitent,
contrite, holy and loving heart,—we are old, and
near our end before we learn that. My brethren,
be no longer children in understanding ; but in
understanding be men.   Think, my brethren,
think. Think your greatest and your best, your
most magnificent, your most deep, and inward, and

spiritual, about God, and about man, made in the
image of God. Think, with all your soul, and heart,
and strength, and mind about the Divine Nature.
Say of the Divine Nature,—" Essence beyond
essence, essence within essence, essence everywhere, and wholly everywhere." Think and say,—
Maker, Nourisher, Guardian, Governor, Benefactor,
and Perfecter of all men and all things. God and
Father: King and Lord: Fountain of Life and
Immortality. Blessed be the glory of the Lord out
of His place. Glory be to Him for His Godhead,
His mysteriousness, His height, His depth, His
sovereignty, His almightiness, His eternity, His
omnipresence, and His grace! Yes, His *omnipresence*, everywhere present, and wholly present
everywhere; but, most of all, and best of all, in
the heart of man. It is in the heart of man that
God establishes His temple. His high throne is
prepared and set up in the heart of man. His holy
altars are builded and kindled in the heart of man.
The sacrifices that alone please God are offered
continually in the heart of man. There, the Holy
Ghost ministers in prayer and praise without
ceasing, making intercession within us with groanings that cannot be uttered. There also is the
golden mercy-seat with the two cherubim above it.
And there the Great High Priest speaketh peace,
and pronounceth His great Benediction, because
He continueth there for ever. Seek thy God, then,

in thyself! Oh, ye sons and daughters of captive
Job, seek Him whom ye have lost, and seek Him in
your own hearts. Come, O prodigal son, come to
thyself. Enter into thyself. Enter deep enough
into thyself, and thou shalt come unto His seat.
For He still sits there, waiting to be gracious there to
thee. Oh, what glory! Oh, what grace! Oh, what
a God! Oh, what a heart! To have thy God in
thine own heart, and to have Him *wholly* there.
Wholly, and not in part; and wholly there for
thee. His whole almightiness, His whole grace and
truth, His whole redemption, His whole salvation!
Arise, then, and enter into God's holy temple.
Order your cause before Him there, and fill your
mouth with your best arguments there. Till you
fall down before Him in your own heart, and say,
"I have heard of Thee by the hearing of the ear:
but now mine eye seeth Thee!"

Are you, then,—by the long-suffering and the
grace of God,—are you one of those who are this
day saying, "Even to-day is my complaint bitter:
my stroke is heavier than my groaning. Oh that
I knew where I might find Him: that I might
come even to His seat!" Then seek Him where
Job sought Him and at last found Him. Seek Him
in a humble, broken, believing heart. Go on seeking Him in a still more, and a still more, humble,
broken, believing heart. Seek Him deep enough,
and long enough: seek Him with your whole

heart ; and sooner, or later, you too will find Him.
Seek Him like David, seven times a day. Like
David also, prevent the night watches and the
dawning of the day seeking Him. If need be, die,
still seeking Him. And die, saying to Him that,
even if He should cast you into your bed in hell,—
warn Him that you will wander about in the outer
darkness for ever seeking Him, and saying : Oh
that I knew where I might find Him : that I might
come even to His seat ! Behold, we count them
happy which endure.

Ye have heard of the patience of Job.

" And the Lord turned the captivity of Job : . . .
and the Lord blessed the latter end of Job more
than his beginning. . . . So Job died, being old and
full of days."

VIII

THE PSALMIST—SETTING THE LORD ALWAYS BEFORE HIM

"Lord, teach us to pray."—LUKE xi. 1.
"I have set the Lord always before me."—Ps. xvi. 8.

IF this so devotionally disposed disciple had lived in the days of David, and if he had asked of David what he here asks of his Master,—that is to say, if he had said to David, "David, thou man after God's own heart, teach me to pray,"—David would have answered him in the words of the text. "Set the Lord before you," David would have said. "Begin every prayer of yours by setting the Lord before you." "I am a companion of all them that fear Thee, and of them that keep Thy precepts," said David. And that made David the most accessible and the most affable of men, especially in divine things. And, accordingly, if you had asked David how he was able to compose such wonderful psalms and prayers,—psalms and prayers that have lasted to this day, and will last as long as the world lasts, and down to the day of judgment,—David would have told you that it was by no power or holiness of his that he did it. "All I

do," he would have said to you, " is just to set the
Lord before me as often as I begin again to sing and
to pray. I begin ; and, ere ever I am aware,
already my prayer is answered, and my psalm is
accepted." " But surely," you would have insisted,
" it must surely have been by very great power and
holiness that such psalms and prayers as the 40th
Psalm, and the 63rd, and the 103rd, and the 119th
were composed. Such psalms and prayers as these
could never have been the composition of a man
subject to like passions as we are." " I remember
well," David would reply, " I shall never forget
just how it was with me the day I began one of
the psalms you have just named. My heart within
me was as a dry and thirsty land that day. But
as I set the Lord before me, and as I went on, I
began to see His power and His glory as I had seen
Him heretofore in His sanctuary, till my soul was
satisfied as with marrow and fatness." If this was
Peter who said to his Master, " Lord, teach us to
pray ! "—and most likely it was—when Peter's
denial of his Master continually came back upon
him in after days he would often go out to David's
sepulchre, which was with them to that day, and
would say in his agony : "David ! David ! David
of the matter of Uriah, and Psalmist of the 51st
Psalm, teach me to pray ! Teach me thy penitential heart. Teach me, the chief of sinners, how
thou didst so praise and so pray." And if David

had still been in the earthly Jerusalem he would have taught Peter to pray by such confidences and confessions as this. " Come, O thou that fearest God," David would have said to Peter, " and I will tell thee what He did for my soul ! After the matter of Uriah, my bones waxed old through my roaring all the day long. Till one day I said, I will confess my transgressions to the Lord ! And I took up my carriages and went a far journey into the wilderness till I came to the Mount of God. And as I ascended the Mount of God, amid lightning and thunder and tempest, with my sin ever before me, the Lord appeared to me and said, ' Behold, there is a place by Me, and thou shalt stand upon a rock . . . and I will cover thee with my hand as I pass by.' And the Lord passed by, and proclaimed, saying, the Lord, the Lord God, merciful and gracious, long-suffering and abundant in goodness and truth. And I made haste and bowed down and said, Forgive mine iniquity, O Lord, and take me for Thy servant. And it was so. And I sang the 103rd Psalm for the first time, all the way home from Horeb to my own house in Jerusalem."

And not the 40th and the 63rd and the 103rd and the 119th Psalms only : but, if you examine with a practised eye any one of the great psalms, you will see that what David says in the text is true of the composition of them all. Whosoever or whatsoever is present or absent from any prayer or psalm of David, the Lord is always present and is never absent. Or if He is ever absent at the beginning of any psalm of David, long before the psalm is ended—and before it has gone far—the Lord is back again at David's right hand. We are allowed to see deep down into David's mind and heart in the composition of some of his psalms. And notably so in the 103rd Psalm. We see David in the opening of that superb psalm calling upon his soul and " all that is within him " to take part in the composition of that superb psalm. And eminent among all that is within David is that so wonderful power he has of setting the Lord before the eyes of his heart. And not David, with his great gifts and great privileges only. But we ourselves,—when we enter our own souls in the same service, we also discover in ourselves the same noble and wonder-working power. By the bodily eye we can set things seen and temporal before ourselves ; but by the spiritual eye we can set before ourselves things unseen and eternal. By our inward eye we are able to see God as we kneel down before Him. We seek His face : and He lifts upon us the light of His countenance sometimes, like the Psalmist, when we " consider the heavens, the work of His fingers, the moon and the stars which He has ordained." We set their Maker and our Maker before us, and we fall down in wonder and in worship saying, How great Thou art, O God ! At another time we cast our

inward eye back on the God of Abraham, and the
God of Isaac and the God of Jacob, and the God
of Moses and Isaiah ; but best of all on the God
and Father of our Lord and Saviour Jesus Christ.
And when we do so, when we set Him before us as
He was revealed to all these sons and servants of
His, then, as we go on doing so, He becomes more
to us than all His creatures ; and Heaven begins
with us to take the place of earth.   Such, even in
this life, do they become who truly " set the Lord
before them " in prayer.   Such do they become
who are taught of David and of Jesus Christ thus
to pray, and thus to praise, and thus to walk with
God, and thus to have their conversation in Heaven.

Our Lord did not say to His disciples in so many
words that they were to set Him, their Master,
always before them when they prayed.   But, all
the same, He meant it.   And after He went away
from them, and went home to His glory, the Holy
Ghost soon made all the apostles see that He had
meant it.   And thus it is that we see, in the Epistles
of Paul and the rest of the Apostles, such a new
departure, so to speak, in prayer.   David's psalms
and prayers are the very best of their kind, and for
their day.   But Paul's prayers are of quite another
kind : they belong to quite another dispensation,
as we say.   There has not been a greater at prayer
and praise, born of women, than David : but the
least New Testament saint is, or he might be, far

greater at prayer than even David. And that, because the least New Testament saint has the Lord Jesus to set before him in prayer, which David, with all his genius, and with all his grace, had not. Everybody must surely see that : even he who never thought about that till this morning—even he must see that " No man hath seen God at any time " : no, not Moses : no, not David. " But the only-begotten Son, who is in the bosom of the Father, He hath declared Him. That which we have seen and heard declare we unto you, that you may have your fellowship with us."

We envy the twelve disciples who saw their Divine Master every day, and had His face and figure printed on their hearts and minds every day. What would we not give just to have seen our Lord's face and figure for once ! To have seen Him when He was blessing the little children, with one of them in His arms ! To have seen His face, and heard His voice, when He spread His skirt over the woman who was washing His feet with her tears ! To have seen and heard His intercessory prayer with His eyes lifted up to Heaven after the supper ! Or, again, when He said, " Father, forgive them ; for they know not what they do ! " It was easy for Peter and James and John to set their Lord always before them ! It was very easy for John to write that he had " an Advocate with the Father," when he remembered so well his Advocate's face, and the

very tones of His voice. I could very easily be
made a believer in Veronica's handkerchief, so much
in this matter is the wish with me father to the
thought ! But no ! Our times are in His hand, and
our lot in this life. And we must not forget that
these are His own words to us on this very matter—
these words—" It is the Spirit that quickeneth :
the flesh profiteth nothing. The words that I speak
unto you, they are Spirit, and they are life."
" Thomas, because thou hast seen Me, thou hast
believed : blessed are they that have not seen, and
yet have believed." And thus it is that the four
evangelists, who had so seen and so handled the
Word of Life, put their book into our hands, saying
as they do so,—these things about our Lord and
yours write we unto you that you may have your
fellowship with us.

Now, if David could set Jehovah always before
him in his prayers and in his psalms,—Jehovah,
Whom no man could see and live,—how much more
should we set Jesus Christ before us ? Jesus
Christ, Who, being the Son of God, became the
Son of Man for this very purpose. And, so we
shall ! For, what state of life is there ?—what
need ? what distress ? what perplexity ? what
sorrow ? what sin ? what dominion and what
disease of sin ? what possible condition can we
ever be in on earth ?—in which we cannot set
Jesus Christ before us in prayer and in faith,

and for help, and for assurance, and for victory ?
Who are you ? and what are you ? and what is
your request and your petition ? Open your
New Testament, take it with you to your knees, and
set Jesus Christ out of it before you. Are you like
David in the 63rd Psalm ? Is your soul thirsting
for God, and is your flesh longing for God in a dry
and thirsty land where no water is ? Then set
Jesus at the well of Samaria before the eyes of your
thirsty heart. And, again, set Him before your
heart when He stood on the last day, that great
day of the feast, and cried, saying, " If any man
thirst let him come to Me and drink." Or, are you
like David after the matter of Uriah ? " For, day
and night, Thy hand was heavy upon me : my
moisture is turned into the drought of summer."
Then set Him before you who says : " I am not
come to call the righteous, but sinners to repentance.
They that be whole need not a physician, but they
that are sick." Or, are you the unhappy father
of a prodigal son ? Then, set your Father in
Heaven always before you : and set the Son of
God always before you as He composes and preaches
the parable of all parables for you and for your
son. Or, are you that son yourself ? Then, never
lie down at night till you have again read that
peculiar parable for you, and set your father and
your mother before you. Or, are you a mother
with a daughter possessed of a devil ? In that

case set Jesus Christ, when He was in the borders
of Tyre and Sidon, before you ; and listen to what
He says to the woman who begged for the crumbs
under the table : The devil, He said to her, is gone
out of thy daughter. Or, are you a happy mother
with your children still, so many little angels in
their innocence and their beauty round about you ?
Then I am sure of you ! You never kiss your
sleeping child, I feel sure, without thinking of Mary,
and how she must have kissed her sleeping child,
and hid all these things in her heart. Or, to come
to a very different kind of person—Are you loaded
with the curses of people who were once in your
cruel power : widows and orphans, and poor and
friendless people ? Then, as often as you remember
their misery and your own—set your Redeemer
before you, who, when He came to the place,
looked up and saw Zacchæus, and said unto him,
" Zacchæus, make haste, and come down : for
to-day I must abide at thy house. . . . This day is
salvation come to this house, forsomuch as he also
is a son of Abraham." Or, again, after twelve
years of many physicians, are you nothing better,
but rather worse ? Then set Him before you till
you are healed of your plague—Him who turned
and said : Who touched Me ? Or are you a minister
with such a message that all your people are walking no more with you ? Then rest your heart on
Him who said to the Twelve, "Will ye also **go**

away ? " And on Him who said on another
occasion, " But other fell into good ground, and
brought forth fruit, some an hundredfold, some
sixtyfold, some thirtyfold." And, O thou afflicted,
tossed with tempest, and not comforted, see Him
coming to the ship, walking on the sea : and see Him,
at another time, in another ship asleep on a pillow :
and hear His rebuke, " O thou of little faith,
wherefore didst thou doubt ? " Or, to come to the
uttermost of all : are you tortured with your own
heart, till you cannot believe that they are worse
tortured in hell itself ? Then look at His face of
infinite pity as He says to His disciples, " For,
from within, out of the heart of men, proceed evil
thoughts, adulteries, fornications, murders, thefts,
covetousness, an evil eye, blasphemy, pride, foolishness : all these evil things come from within." And,
if there is any other manner of man here, for whose
soul no man cares, let that man set the Good
Shepherd before him as He says : " I am the door ;
by Me if any man enter in he shall go in and out,
and find pasture." And, again, " Come unto Me, all
ye that labour and are heavy laden, and I will give
you rest." Sinners ! set your Saviour always
before you ! Child of God ! set your Father in
Heaven, and His Son from Heaven, always before
you ! And, because They are at your right hand,
you shall not be greatly moved.

And, then, He has appointed special times, and

special places, and special circumstances, and special
accompaniments of prayer : at which times, in
which places, and amid which accompaniments
and circumstances He will be specially present, and
will in an especial manner set Himself before you.
Seize those golden, but irrecoverable opportunities ;
seize them so that He shall never be able to say to
you that He never knew you. His own word, for
one. Never open the New Testament till you have
said to yourself : " Now, O my soul, let us proceed
no further till we have set Him of Whom we are now
to read before us ! " Never hear a chapter of the
Gospel read without seeing, as if you had been there,
all that is read about. Be for the time, in Bethlehem,
and in Nazareth, and in Galilee, and in Jerusalem,
and in the Garden, and on Golgotha, and on Olivet.
Never see His Name even in pen or pencil, and
never hear His Name in a sermon, or in a psalm or
prayer, without seeing His face at the same time
and falling down before Him. And when you are
in your own place of prayer, do not be in a hurry
to get on with your prayer and to get done with it.
If need be, He can make the sun stand still to give
you time to pray. Never kneel without at the same
time shutting your eyes on all earthly things, and
setting God on His Throne in Heaven, and Jesus
Christ in His intercession, before you. Take time.
It is lost time to speak to the wall. Take time till
you are quite sure that you have His ear. Be

silent till you have something to say. And then, say it not into the air, but into the ear and the heart of Jesus Christ. For He has an ear and a heart too, and they are both, if you like, open to you. You are at family worship, say, and you open your hymn-book, and you come on John Newton's sweet hymn :

> How sweet the name of Jesus sounds
> In a believer's ear !

Yes, but does it at that moment sound sweet in your ear ? Are you that believer ? And is your ear full in a moment, of an unearthly sweetness ? You are a believer, and your ear is full of that sweetness, when you set the Owner of that Name always before you.

> Jesus, my Shepherd, Husband, Friend !

and on the spot you are a lost sheep, a woman forsaken and a friendless outcast—all met, all satisfied, and all aglow with the love of Christ shed abroad in your heart.

> My Prophet, Priest and King !

and all that is within you is that moment at His feet !

> My Lord, my Life, my Way, my End,
> Accept the praise I bring :

and the praise you bring is all, at that moment, accepted ; and all because you did set the Lord before you.

You remember what is told of that old saint who so set the cross and its bleeding Burden before

him, that the five wounds actually came down from
off the Cross, and printed themselves on his hands
and on his feet and on his side.   It is a parable of
what takes place every day in every true saint of
God and disciple of Christ.   They set their dying
Lord always before them till they are crucified with
Him and till they bear about in the body the dying
of the Lord Jesus.   Join the great saints in this
their crucifixion with Christ.   My brethren, set the
Lord Jesus on His Cross and on His Throne before
you in all your psalms, in all your prayers, in all
your Scriptures, and at all times, till He is ever with
you : and till it would not surprise you to feel His
hand laid on your head, and to look up and see His
face some night-watch as you so abide before Him.
Set your Lord, in all these ways, before you, till,
suddenly, some midnight soon, the Bridegroom is
with you and you are for ever with Him!   Even so,
come quickly, Lord Jesus!

IX

HABAKKUK—ON HIS WATCH-TOWER

"Lord, teach us to pray."—LUKE xi. 1.

"I will stand upon my watch, and set me upon the tower."—HAB. ii. 1.

HABAKKUK's tower was not built of stone and lime Hiram's Tyrian workmen, with all their skill in hewn stone, and in timber, and in iron, and in brass, had no hand in building Habakkuk's tower. "The Name of the Lord" was Habakkuk's high tower. The truth and the faithfulness and the power of God—these things were the deep and broad foundations of Habakkuk's high tower, into which he continually escaped, and from the high top of which he was wont to look out upon the land, and up to his God. God's grace and mercy and long-suffering were the doors and stairs, were the walls and battlements, of Habakkuk's high tower; and God's sure salvation was the golden and the far-shining roof of it. "Art Thou not from everlasting,"—prayed this prophet as often as he again stood upon his watch and set himself upon his tower,—"O Lord, my God, mine Holy One? We shall **not** die."

The Chaldeans had, by this time, overrun the
whole land. Judah and Jerusalem had for long
been full of all but unpardonable sin. God's chosen
and covenant people had despised and forsaken God.
The law of God was " slacked," till the land was full
of all unrighteousness. And thus it was that this
judgment of God had already gone forth against
Judah and Jerusalem : " Lo, I raise up the Chaldeans, that bitter and hasty nation, which shall
march through the breadth of the land, to possess
the dwelling-places that are not theirs. They are
terrible and dreadful. . . . Their horses also are
swifter than the leopards, and are more fierce than
the evening wolves : . . . they shall fly as the eagle
that hasteth to eat. They shall come all for violence :
. . . and they shall gather the captivity as the
sand." And it was so. It was very much as if the
Turks of our day had been let loose on England,
and Scotland, and Edinburgh. It was amid the
indescribable cruelties and horrors of the invasion
and possession of Judah and Jerusalem by the
Chaldeans that Habakkuk took up his burden.
And Habakkuk the prophet was alone : he was
alone, and had no fellow in the midst of all those
desolate years. Alone !—and with his faith very
hard pressed between God, in His righteous anger
on the one hand, and guilty Judah, under her great
agony and oppression, on the other hand. And we
have this great and noble-hearted prophet in all the

heat and burden of his work,—in his faith, and in his prayer, and in his songs,—all set before us with extraordinary beauty and impressiveness in this wonderful little book : a book little in size, indeed, but a book rich and great in divine substance, and in intellectual and spiritual power of every kind. " O Lord, how long shall I cry, and Thou wilt not hear ! even cry out unto Thee of violence, and Thou wilt not save ! Why dost Thou shew me iniquity, and cause me to behold grievance ? For spoiling and violence are before me: . . . and the wicked doth compass about the righteous . . . but I will stand upon my watch, and I will set me upon the tower, and I will watch to see what He will say to me. . . . And the Lord answered me and said, Write the vision, and make it plain upon tables, that he may run that readeth it." And, at that, the prophet immediately came down from his tower ; and had great tablets made by the workman; and he wrote this text upon the tables,—this text, " The just shall live by his faith." And he had the tables hung up on the temple walls, and on the gates and on the market-places of the city ; till he who ran from the oppression of the enemy, as well as he who ran to take up arms against the oppressor, might read the legend,—this legend,—that " The just shall live by his faith." The Chaldeans understood not the tables, but the oppressed people of God understood them ; till it abides a proverb, and an encourage-

ment, and a doctrine, and a sure hope to this day,—
that " The just shall live by faith."

1. In a profound and far-reaching passage,—in
two profound and far-reaching passages indeed,—
Pascal impresses on us, out of such Scripture as this,
that our own passions are our only enemies. Our
real enemies, with all their cruelty and all their
oppression, come up upon us,—not out of Chaldea,
but out of our own heart Chaldea, with all her
cruel and aggrandising ambition, would never have
been allowed to cross the Jordan and let loose in
Judah, but for Judah's sin. And it was Judah's
continuing transgression and persisting impeni-
tence that kept the Chaldeans in possession of
Judah and Jerusalem. All which is written in the
prophet, with Pascal's profound and spiritual interpretation of the prophet, for our learning, and
for our very closest and most practical application
to ourselves. Let this, then, be laid to heart by
all God's people, that their sinful hearts, and sinful
lives, while they are in this present life, are always,
more or less, like the land of Judah under the cruel
occupation of the Chaldeans. Our sins, my
brethren, have brought the bitterest of all our
chastisements upon us, that is, upon our souls. Not
every child of God among us has yet spirituality of
mind enough, or personal experience enough, to see
and to admit that. Judah did not easily and willingly see and admit that. But Habakkuk in his

day, and Pascal in our day, saw it : they both saw
it ; and wrote powerfully and convincingly and
with splendid comfort concerning it. And many
of God's people among yourselves, by much experience, by much prayer, by a sinful heart and a
holy life taken together, are themselves prophets,—
prophets and philosophers : wise men, that is, in
the deepest things, both of God, and of the soul of
man. And one of those deepest things is just this
—that *God chastises sin by means of sin.* He
employs the remaining sinfulness of the sanctified
heart as His last and His best instrument for
reaching down into the depths of the heart in order
to its complete discovery, complete correction, and
complete purification. There is no tyranny so
terrible, there is no invasion and captivity of the
soul one-thousandth part so horrible, and so hated
of all God's saints, as is their captivity to their own
sins   Those whose true torments and tortures come,
never from without, but always from within : those
whose abidingly bad hearts are being made God's
cruellest scourge,—both for their past sins, and
for their present sinfulness,—*they* will consent and
subscribe to all that this great prophet says in the
terrible account that he gives of the Chaldeans.
" That bitter and hasty nation : which march
through the breadth of the land, to possess dwelling-
places that are not theirs. They are terrible and
dreadful." " They are proud : they enlarge their

desire like hell : they are as death itself : they
cannot be satisfied. . . . Shall they not rise up
suddenly that shall bite thee ? And awake that
shall vex thee ? And thou shalt be for a booty to
them, O Jerusalem ! " All of which is but a cruel
parable to some of us concerning our own sins. So
truly does our God also, in His grace and truth,
still make His own so sovereign, and so spiritual,
use of our remaining and deep-rooted sinfulness. In
His wisdom, and in His love, at one stroke, He does
these two divinest of things :—securing the greatest
depth, the greatest inwardness and the greatest
spirituality for our sanctification ; and, at the same
time, securing, more and more every day, our fear
and hatred and horror at our own hearts, as at
nothing else on earth or in hell. Is that your mind,
my brethren ? Is that your experience ? " The
spiritual understood Chaldea of their passions," says
Pascal. " The unspiritual, and the still carnal-
minded, understood it of Chaldea only. The term
' enemy,' " he adds, "and Chaldea is obscure and
ambiguous only to the unspiritual in mind and in
heart." Let all students of Holy Scripture, and of
the heart of man, study Pascal.

2. Look, now, at that man of God, who is like
Habakkuk in our own days. Look at that prophet
upon his tower in our own city. He has climbed
up far above us, his fellows, into a calm and clear
air : and he has so climbed by means of much

prayer, and by means of much meditation, and by means of much secret self-denial of many kinds. He has a time and a place of retreat, and of purification, and of exaltation of mind, that we know nothing of. He may be a minister ; most likely he is : or he may be a busy business man, as sometimes he is. He may be well known to us to be a man like Habakkuk : or, he may be hidden even from himself. Sometimes he is old : and, not seldom, he is young. In any case, he is our Habakkuk. Habakkuk, with his own burden, and sometimes with ours. " O Lord," he cries on his watch, " how long shall I cry, and Thou wilt not hear !" " But I will stand upon my watch, and set me upon the tower, and will watch to see what He will say unto me." There are men among us who do not neglect prayer, who yet sadly neglect to watch and wait for God's promised answer to their prayers. Prayer, when we think of it, and perform it aright,— prayer is a magnificent thing—and a venturesome, —for any man to do. For prayer builds, and fits out, and mans, and launches a frail vessel of faith on the deep and wide sea of God's sovereignty : and sets her sails for a harbour nothing short of heaven. And, then, the wise merchantman gives God, and his ship, time to be on her way back again : and then, like Habakkuk, he sets himself on his high tower. All his interests are now up there. As Paul has it—all his conversation is in heaven :

all his treasures and all his affections are launched
on that sea-adventure he is now so intensely watching up there. I am convinced, my brethren, that
we lose many answers to our prayers,—not so
much because we do not pray, as because we do not
go up to our tower to watch for and to welcome
God's answers to our prayers. " Why should I
answer ? "—our God may well say to His waiting
and ministering angels. " Why should I answer
him ? He pays no attention to My answer to his
prayer. He is never on his watch, when I send My
answer. And, even when I do send My answers to
his house and to his heart, he takes them and holds
them as common and everyday things. He never
wonders at My grace to him. He never performs
his vow for My goodness to him. He holds a
thousand,—he and his—of My benefits : but he
does not seem to know it." My brethren, I am
as sure as I am standing here, that we would all
get far more, and far more wonderful answers to
prayer, if only we were far more on the outlook for
them. Habakkuk never made a holier or a more
fruitful resolve than when he said, " I will stand
upon my watch, and set me upon the tower, and
will watch to see what He will say unto me."

3. There were many shapes and sizes of towers in
the land of Judah, and they were put, of the people
of Judah and Jerusalem, to many and various
uses. Their city walls would rise up, all round their

cities, into strong towers, both for defence and for
beauty. Immense towers were built also by the
military engineers of those days on frontiers, and
on passes, and on peaks, and on exposed situations.
To protect a great well also, a strong stone tower
would be built, so as to secure safety to the flocks
of cattle and sheep that came to the well and to its
waters to drink. No vineyard worth anything to
its owner was ever left without its tower,—both to
lodge the keeper of the vineyard, and to be the home
of the grape-gatherers at the grape-gathering
season. Till, all over the land, and all round the
city, all kinds of towers stood up to give life, and
strength, and beauty to the whole landscape.

And so it is in the Church of Christ. Till He who
sees His own holy land as no eye but His sees it :
He who sees every soldier and watchman, and
vinedresser, and keeper of sheep, in it : He who
has His sleepless eye on every praying and expect-
ing soul,—He sees His Holy Land, and His Holy
City, encompassed, and ramparted, and orna-
mented with ten thousand such towers : and He
never long leaves any such tower without its proper
and appointed vision. For, as often as any watching soul says, " I will stand upon my watch, and
will set me upon my tower," the Lord who spake
to Habakkuk says to us the same thing : " Though
it tarry, wait for it ; because it will surely come, it
will not tarry." And, there is nothing that our

Lord says so often as just *this*,—He says it every morning, indeed, and every night to all who wait for Him,—" *The just*," He says without ceasing, " *shall live by his faith*." Till one tower answers that vision, that password and watchword, to another; till all the land rings with it, and echoes with it. The Lord speaks it first to Habakkuk, and Habakkuk to Paul, and Paul to Rome and Galatia, and Rome and Galatia to us; and still the same counsel and comfort keeps on counselling all the dwellers in their lonely towers, " The just shall live by faith." What Habakkuk wrote six hundred years before Christ on the gates, and walls, and pillars of Jerusalem—that very same word of God the Holy Spirit of God is writing on the tables that are in the believing hearts of all God's people still : " Being justified by faith we have peace with God ": " By grace ye are saved through faith ": " The just shall live by his faith." He shall live,—not so much by the fulfilment of all God's promises ; nor by God's full answers to his prayers and expectations ; nor by the full deliverance of his soul from his bitter enemies ; nor by the full and final expulsion of the Chaldeans : but he shall live, amid all these troubles, and till they come to an end for ever,—he shall live by his firm faith in God, and in the future which is all in God's hand. And thus it is that, whatever our oppression and persecution may be. whatever our prayer and wherever and

whatever our waiting tower, still this old and ever
new vision and answer comes : Faith : Faith : and
Faith only. Rest and trust in God. Commit thy
way to God. Be thine enemy from beyond the
Euphrates, or be he out of the evil of thine own
heart,—keep on in prayer. Keep on watching.
Keep thyself on thy Tower. Keep saying, keep
singing :

> For thou art God that dost
> To me salvation send,
> And I upon Thee all the day
> Expecting do attend.

Go up every new day into Habakkuk's high
tower. And take up his prayer and his hope. Art
Thou not from everlasting, O Lord, my God, mine
Holy One ? I shall not die. Say *you* also, " I shall
not die." *That* is faith. *That* is the very faith by
which the just have been enabled to live in all ages
of the Church of God. No man ever died under
the hand of his enemy who *so* believed in God, and
in the power and grace of God. You may sometimes be afraid that you are to be left to die in your
sin and sorrow. So was Habakkuk sometimes.
" O Lord, I heard Thy speech, and was afraid."
Habakkuk was afraid to face the whole long, unbroken, unrelieved life of faith, and of *faith only*.
Habakkuk would be up on his tower again to see
if there were no signs of the Chaldeans leaving the
land. At another time he would stand upon his
tower, and look if none of Judah's old alliances

were coming to her help. But still the full vision
of his salvation tarried, till he came to seek his
salvation, not in any outward thing whatsoever;
not even in complete deliverance from the Chaldeans, but in GOD,—whether the Chaldeans were
in possession of Judah, and Jerusalem, or driven
out of it. Till, taught of God, as he dwelt more and
more with God in his high tower, Habakkuk was
able to rise and attain to this,—to this which is
one of the highest attainments of faith, and hope,
and love in all the Old Testament,—" Yet I will
rejoice in the Lord, I will joy in the God of my
salvation. The Lord God is my strength, and He
will make my feet like hinds' feet, and He will make
me to walk upon mine high places."

4. The Chaldeans with all their overwhelming
invasions, and with all their cruel oppressions, have,
then, been made Habakkuk's salvation. "They
took possession of dwelling-places that were not
theirs": till Habakkuk was compelled to seek a
dwelling-place that even they, with all their horses
like leopards, and all their horsemen like evening
wolves, could not invade. They had hunted
Habakkuk all his life, up into his high tower, till he
is now far more of his time in his high tower than
he is on the street, or even in the temple of Jerusalem. And till, at last, Habakkuk has come to
this, that he asks for no more in this world but to be
let *walk* on his " high place " into which he has been

wont so often to climb. In Paul's seraphic words, Habakkuk's whole conversation is now in heaven. He has gone up upon his high tower so often, and has set himself for such long seasons on his watch, that he is now far more in heaven than on earth. Habakkuk will not only, all his remaining days, "watch" and "wait" on his high tower, but Habakkuk will *walk* there. He will *dwell* there. His true home and his sure dwelling-place will be up *there*. Till, when the "beatific vision" comes,—which will soon come to Habakkuk, and will not tarry, — it will find him walking, and waiting for it on his high places. " If ye then be risen with Christ, seek those things which are above, where Christ sitteth on the right hand of God. Set your affection on things above, and not on things on the earth. . . . When Christ, who is our Life, shall appear, then shall ye also appear with Him in glory."

X

OUR LORD—SANCTIFYING HIMSELF

" Lord, teach us to pray."—LUKE xi. 1.
" And for their sakes I sanctify Myself . . ."—JOHN xvii. 19.

" I HAVE an exceedingly complex idea of sanctification," says John Wesley in his Journal. And that
must surely be an exceedingly complex sanctification, pursuit, attainment and experience which
embraces both our Lord and all His disciples,—
both Him who knew no sin, and those disciples of
His who know nothing but sin.

But what exactly is sanctification ? What is
sanctification both in its complexity and in its
simplicity ? Well, " Sanctification," according to
the Catechism, " is the work of God's free grace,
whereby we are renewed in the whole man, after
the image of God, and are enabled, more and more,
to die unto sin, and to live unto righteousness."
Now, to begin with, in all the complexity and completeness of our Lord's sanctification, could He have
subscribed to that catechism ? Could He have
signed what all our deacons sign ? When He
examined Himself before every approaching passover, would He have found all that going forward

within Himself? Yes,—most certainly, He would,
every single syllable of it. For it was of His
Father's " free grace " that He, the man Christ
Jesus, the carpenter's son, was what He was, and
did what He did. He was " renewed in the whole
man " also, ere ever He was a man. And for thirty
years, this, our Lord's sanctification, grew in all
its complexity and completeness till He was mani-
fested to Israel as the very Image of God among
men. And, while all His days " dead to sins," He
was enabled more and more every day to die to sin
and to " live unto righteousness," till in the text,
and within a few hours of His death on the cross,
He is still sanctify ng Himself—that is, surrendering
Himself, dedicating Himself, devoting Himself, to
fulfil and to finish His Father's will, and to accom-
plish the salvation of all whom the Father hath
given Him. " For their sakes I sanctify Myself ;
that they also might be sanctified through the
truth."

It was only after an immense " complexity " of
ceremonial, indeed, but also of moral and spiritual
sanctification, that the high priest in Israel was able
to enter the Holy of Holies, there to make acceptable
intercession for the people. And in the whole of
this great intercessory prayer of our Lord, and in
the whole of the corresponding Epistle to the
Hebrews, we see through what an inwardness and
spirituality and "complexity," both of personal

and of official sanctification, our Lord was prepared, and made perfect, for His crowning office of our Great High Priest. The angel Gabriel described Him as " that holy thing " before He was born. " For such an high priest became us, who is holy, harmless, undefiled, separate from sinners, and made higher than the heavens." In His own words, and with His eyes lifted up to heaven : " Father, the hour is come : and for their sakes,"—looking round on the Eleven,—" I sanctify Myself."

Now, here again, my brethren,—for it meets us at every turn,—as He was, so are we, in our measure, in this world. As many of us, that is, as are chosen, and called, and ordained, and anointed for the sake of other men, as well as for our own sake. We are to be God's remembrancers on the earth. We are to be men of prayer, and especially of inter- cessory prayer. We are to be, for a time, in this world, that which our Lord is everlastingly in heaven. We are to be kings and priests unto God and His Father by the blood of the Lamb. As He was sanctified, as He sanctified Himself, for their sake, so is it to be with us. As He was in His life of holiness, and consequent intercession, so are we to be in this world. We must sanctify ourselves for the sake of others. We must *first* sanctify ourselves, and *then* pray, first for ourselves, and then for others. And that is not our Lord's command and example only. Apart from all that, it stands to reason, and it stands to experience. Every kind of prayer, not intercessory prayer only, which is the highest kind of prayer, but all prayer, from the lowest kind to the highest, is impossible in a life of known and allowed sin. The blind man's retort upon the Pharisees is his retort upon us to this day,—" Now we know that God heareth not sinners." No ! No man's prayer is acceptable with God whose life is not well-pleasing before God. The very ploughing of the wicked is sin. We all know that in ourselves. The man in this house with the least and the lowest religious experience,— he has enough in himself to convince him that sin and prayer cannot both live at the same time in the same heart. Admit sin, and you banish prayer. But, on the other hand, entertain, and encourage, and practise prayer, and sin will sooner or later flee before it : and entertain and practise *intercessory* prayer, and you will, by degrees, and in process of time, sanctify yourself to an inwardness and to a spirituality, and to a complexity, and to a simplicity that hitherto you have had no experience of, no conception of, and indeed no ambition after.

Now, having said " ambition,"—Who has this holy ambition ? Who has the ambition to be bound up in the bundle of life with the Saviour of men ? Who has the high heart to shine at last as the brightness of the firmament, and as the stars for ever and ever ? Are you able to drink of your Lord's

cup of sanctification, so as to sit with Him on His
throne ?   Are you willing to wear, not only the ring
and the shoes of a returning prodigal, but, in addi-
tion, the crown and the mitre of a king and a priest
unto God ?   Then,—take this text out of your
Lord's mouth, and make it henceforth your own.
Look at Him ! Look every day at Him ! Never
take your eyes off Him ! " Lift your eyes to
heaven " — just like Him; and, like Him, say,
as He said that great night of sanctification and
prayer, " Father, Holy Father ! For their sakes I
also sanctify myself."

The first human ears these wonderful words ever
fell on were the ears of the Eleven.   Their Master
had chosen the Eleven to be the future preachers of
the Gospel, and pastors of the flock.   They heard all
their Lord's words, both of counsel and of comfort,
and of prayer that night ; only, they did not understand what they heard.   But, after their Master's
Crucifixion, and Resurrection, and Ascension, and
after the Pentecostal Outpouring of the Holy Spirit
—then, all these things came back to their understanding and their remembrance.   And, as time
went on, there was nothing in that Great Prayer
the Apostles remembered more in their daily ministry
than just this : " For their sakes I sanctify Myself."
They remembered these words every day, and they
saw something of the unfathomable and inexhaustible
depth of these words, as they worked out their

own salvation, and the salvation of their people, in a daily life of increasing holiness and intercessory prayer. And those ministers of our own day are the true successors of the Eleven, who most closely imitate them in their life of sanctification : and that, with a view to intercessory prayer. He alone deserves to be called a minister of Christ and of His Church who, on the day of his ordination, looks round on his people, and says,—" For their sakes I sanctify myself ; " and more and more says it with every returning Sabbath morning. "For their sakes," he will say, " I dedicate and devote myself. For their sakes I keep myself at peace with God. For their sakes I practise the Presence of God. I seek more and more to please God for their sakes. To please Him and to please them. For their sakes I sanctify myself." And, what an incomparable sanctification that is, and what a shipwreck it is for any minister to miss it ! What a complex, what a spiritual, what an endless, what an incessant sanctification ! In every new sermon there is some new sanctification for a preacher, and for his people. First and best for him ; and, then, after him, for them. "Sanctify them through Thy truth : Thy word is truth." In every pastoral visit, at every sick-bed, at every death-bed, at every open grave, what a complex sanctification for a true minister every day ! And, then, every night, what a correspondingly complex intercession for his people !

Every man in his congregation,—little known to
the man himself,—has some new and secret and
stolen sanctification hidden about him for his
minister.   Every man's humility, lowliness of mind,
and love : every man's rudeness, ill-nature, in-
gratitude, and insolence, hardness to move, stubborn-
ness to turn, pride not to be told the truth.   And,
in the face of all that, a minister's own folly, ignor-
ance, unteachableness, offensiveness, idleness,—
and all the other vices of the ministerial heart
and life and office.   Men and brethren, what a
complex, what a splendid sanctification is here !
Not for you.   At any rate, not immediately for
you : but for your ministers ; and, then, through
their consequent intercessions, for you.   What a
scope !   What a field !   What an opportunity !
For *that* man's sake, what meekness and humility
in his minister !   For *that* man's sake, what forgiveness and long-suffering !   For *that* man's sake,
what courage and boldness !   And for *that* man's
sake, what patience and what hope against hope !
And for *all* men's sakes, what self-condemnation
and constant contrition of heart !   But who is
sufficient for all these things ?   Who but he that
has something of the mind and experience of Christ
as to the universality, and the malignity, and the
irremediableness of sin ; as also of the power of
prayer, and prayer out of a holier and an ever-holier
life ?   O young men !   O gifted young men !   O

ambitious young men! O courageous and great-hearted young men! Choose the pulpit for your life-work! Choose the pastorate! Choose, and endure to the end in this incomparable sanctification. Only, rather beg your bread, rather break stones on the roadside than enter the ministry, unless you are determined to know nothing, day nor night, but to sanctify yourselves for their sakes!

But, almost more than any minister, let every father and mother among us see to it that they make this blessed Scripture the law and the rule of their family life. Let very Nature herself come in here to supplement and to strengthen grace. Let all fathers, and all mothers, look round upon their families every day, and say together before God : For their sakes we sanctify ourselves. Every father and mother makes daily intercession before God in the behalf of their children. But, if they would succeed in that, they must do more than that. They must add sanctification to intercession. They must learn of Christ the true secret of His intercessory and prevailing prayer. They must lay this too long-neglected text to heart,—" For their sakes I sanctify myself."

What is it that makes you pray with such secret tears for that son of yours ? What is it that makes you so remorseful as you see him growing up so fast in your house, and not at the same time growing in grace, and in wisdom, and in the favour of God ?

Is it not that you cannot but see so much of yourself
in your ill-fated son? So much of your own
wilfulness and selfishness, and pride, and bad temper,
and incipient sensuality, and what not. It is what
he has inherited from you that causes you such
remorse, sometimes, that ever he was begotten of
you. It is this that makes you pray for yourself,
and for him, with such passionate importunity. All
that is well; but even all that is not enough. Have
you ever tried sanctification,—self-sanctification,—
upon your son, upon yourself, and upon God?
Try still more sanctification of yourself, before you
despair, and give up hope. I say it in His house
and in His presence: and He will speak out, and
will contradict it if it is not true. *God cannot resist
a parent's prayer when it is sufficiently backed up
with a parent's sanctification.* I say it to you, in
His hearing, that, though He will not answer your
most importunate prayer by itself: yet, because
of your sanctification added to it, He will say to
you: Be it unto you all that you will! Make
experiment by still more sanctification. Sanctify,
clean out of yourself, all that it so pains and con-
founds you to see reproduced in your son. Con-
temporaneously with your prayers and your counsels,
carry you on a secret assault both upon God and
upon your son through a still more secret and a
still more complete sanctification of yourself. Leave
nothing undone so that all your prayers and all

your reproofs may have their full and unbroken force, both upon God and upon your son.

It is a very fine sight to see a father taking on a new, and a better, and a more modern education alongside of his son. What a happy household that is when a father is open to all his sons' tutors and schoolmasters both in nature, and in providence, and in grace—the father and the son still keeping step together in the great school of life. That is wise, and noble, and beautiful, and very fruitful. Now, let all fathers, in like manner, sanctify themselves through their sons. Let them modernise and freshen up, and carry on, and complete their *sanctification* also, seeing themselves as in a glass, in their son's sin and salvation. It is supremely for this that God setteth His solitaries in families. It is of such a family that the prophet speaks when all the rest of the earth has been smitten with a curse. All the earth, that is, but that house where the heart of the father has been turned to the child, and the heart of the child to the father : that house in which the father says, in the words of the text,—" For the sake of my son I will sanctify myself."

It is altogether too dreadful to speak about— the " curse " with which God smites some unsanctified fathers. And, who can tell, among so many fathers here, but that curse may not have begun to fall ? There may be a hidden horror in

some father's heart here that he does not, and cannot
love his son, as all other fathers are blessed in loving
their sons, and in their sons loving them. Such a
man feels himself to be a monster among fathers.
Your son has grown up to manhood in the house of
an unsanctified and an unprayerful father. And,
as was prophesied in a thousand scriptures, and
seen in a thousand of your neighbours' houses,—
as a father sows in his son, so shall he reap. You
took your own way with God, and your son is now
taking his own way with you. You despised God's
counsels, and all that your son has done has been
to despise yours. " If I am a father," you say,
" where is mine honour ? " But God said that
first, and said it about you. Try the deliverance
of the text before you absolutely destroy yourself.
You have done everything a father can do, you say.
No, you have not sanctified yourself. Try sanctification upon God, and upon yourself, and upon your
son. Die this very day to your proud heart ; and
having begun to die, so die daily. " O Almighty
God ! O God of all grace ! Pity a most miserable
man ! Sanctify me : break me to pieces : melt
me to tears : do what Thou wilt with me : do all
that I need to have done : only, if it be possible,
take this hell out of my heart, and give me back
my lost love for my child, and his for me ! "

Till your neighbours—instead of loud and angry
words—will hear the voice of Psalms in the taber-

nacles of the righteous : " For He hath torn, and He will heal us ; He hath smitten, and He will bind us up." Sanctify yourself, then, from all the remaining dregs of pride, and anger, and temper, and tyranny in your heart and life, as also from all those appetites that inflame and exasperate all these evil things. Sanctify yourself to please God, and to pacify conscience, and wait and see what God will do to you in His pity and in His love. He has no pleasure in the death of the wicked : make you, therefore, a new heart, and a new spirit, saith the Lord. Sanctify yourself ; and wait and see.

There is perhaps not one of us come to years, who has not some child or some other relation ; some old schoolfellow or college friend ; some partner in business ; or some companion in sin, or some one else, that we are compelled from time to time to pray for, as we see them going down in sickness, or in poverty, or in vice, or it may be even in crime. Men differ greatly in the tenderness and in the pain of their hearts and their consciences in such cases. But we all know something, no doubt, of this remorse and this horror at the ruin and the misery of men we once knew so well. It is many years since you have even seen him. You did what you could to assist him ; and since then you have tried hard to wash your hands of him. But, like the cock-crowing, which, as often as Peter again heard it anywhere to the end of his life, always called

back to his unhappy mind his denial of his Master :
so there are things that you cannot help hearing,
that call back your long past to your conscience.
Your conscience may be very unreasonable and
very unjust,—but be quiet she will not. " Thou art
the man ! but for thee that poor shipwreck might
to this day have been a happy and a prosperous
and a good man." I cannot tell you the terrible
shock a case of that kind gave to myself last week.
There is a man still in this life I had neglected to
pray for, for a long time past. Days and weeks,—
and I never once mentioned his name. I used to
sanctify myself for his sake : but daily self-denial
is uphill work with me ; and I had insensibly slipped
out of it. But, as God would have it, a letter came
into my hands last week, that called back my
present text to my mind. I may not tell you all
that was in that letter, but the very postmark made
my heart to stand still. And as I opened the letter
and read it,—Shall I tell you what I felt ? I felt
as if I had murdered my old friend. I felt as if he
had been drowned, while, all the time, I had refused
to throw him the rope that was in my hand. I felt
his blood burning like vitriol on my soul. And a
voice cried after me on the street, and would not be
silent even in my sleep, " Thou art the man ! " I
could get no rest till I had resolved, and had begun
to *sanctify myself* again unto importunate prayer
for his sake. To deny myself, to watch unto prayer,

and to take his name, night and day, back to God.
" I cannot let Thee go unless Thou dost save that
man : if he is lost, how can my name be found in
Thy Book ? "   How I will persevere and succeed,
in my future sanctification for his sake,—I cannot
tell.   The *event* alone will tell !   At any rate, I
have preached this sermon this morning out of my
own heartsore experience, as well as out of this
great intercessory text.

XI

OUR LORD IN THE GARDEN

' Lord, teach us to pray."—LUKE xi. 1.
" Then cometh Jesus with them unto a place called Gethsemane, and saith unto the disciples, Sit ye here, while I go and
pray yonder."—MATT. xxvi. 36.

> Gethsemane can I forget ?
> Or there Thy conflict see,
> Thine agony and bloody sweat,—
> And not remember Thee ?

" THEN cometh Jesus with them unto a place called
Gethsemane," says Matthew, who was one of them.
" And when they had sung an hymn, they went out
into the Mount of Olives," says Mark. " And He
came out," writes Luke, " and went, as He was
wont, to the Mount of Olives ; and His disciples
also followed Him." And, then, John, who also was
one of them, has it thus : " When Jesus had spoken
these words, He went forth with His disciples over
the brook Cedron, where was a garden, into the
which He entered, and His disciples. And Judas
also, which betrayed Him, knew the place ; for
Jesus ofttimes resorted thither with His disciples."
Where our version says " a *place* called Gethsemane," the Vulgate version has " a villa " : while

the Rheims version has in Matthew " a country place," and in Mark " a farm "—" a farm called Gethsemane." Now, there was in Gethsemane a garden, and the owner of that garden had given our Lord full permission to come and go in that garden when and where He pleased. Make yourself at home in my garden, said the owner of Geth-semane to our Lord ; and He did so. " It was His wont to go out to that garden," says one of the evangelists. " He ofttimes resorted thither," says another.

When he is leading his readers up to all this, Luke, with his practised pen, has two verses that throw a flood of light on the whole of that Passover week, so full of preaching and of prayer. " And in the daytime He was teaching in the temple ; and at night He went out, and abode in the mount that is called the Mount of Olives. And all the people came early in the morning to Him in the temple, for to hear Him." We have some of the sermons of that Passover week preserved to this day in the 21st, 22nd, 23rd, 24th and 25th of Matthew ; and terrible sermons they must have been. They are sufficiently terrible to read to this day : and what must they have been to hear that week, and to hear from the lips of the Lamb ! So terrible was His preaching that Passover week that it did more than anything else to bring matters to a head, and to a last issue, between the preacher and His enemies. If true preaching does not subdue us, it is sure to exasperate us. The better the preaching is, the more it is either a savour of life or a savour of death to him who hears it. " This was but a matter of seven days before He was crucified," says Dr. Thomas Goodwin, one of the savouriest of the Puritan preachers. " For, Christ when He saw that He must die, and that now His time was come, He wore His body out : He cared not, as it were, what became of Him : He wholly spent Himself in preaching all day, and in praying all night " : preaching in the temple those terrible parables, and praying in the garden such prayers as the 17th of John, and " Thy will be done ! " even to a bloody sweat.

" And they came to a place which was named Gethsemane : and He saith to His disciples, Sit ye here, while I shall pray. And He taketh with Him Peter and James and John. . . . And He was withdrawn from them about a stone's-cast, and kneeled down, and prayed." Now, if you knew to a certainty that your last agony was to come upon you this Sabbath night ; if all your past sins were this very night to find you out, and to be laid of God and man upon you—before morning—how many of us would you take with you ? Christ took His eleven disciples—but He soon saw that they were far too many. Till He selected three, and said to the rest, " Tarry ye here." Who of us,

and how many of us would you send for to-night,
if you knew to a certainty that the wine-cup of the
wrath of God was to be put into your hands to-
night ?   Would you take your minister and your
elder, and who else to make up the three ?   John
Knox took his wife and said to her, " Read to me
that Scripture on which I first cast my anchor."
Have you a wife, or a mother, or a brother, or a
friend who sticketh closer to you than your brother,
whom you could let come within a stone's-cast of
your soul, when your agony was upon you ?   No.
Not one.   We should all have to stand back when
the heaviness and the exceeding sorrow, and the
amazement and the great agony came, and the
bloody sweat.

> Down to Gehenna, and up to the throne,
> He travels the fastest, who travels alone.

" And He began to be sorrowful, and very heavy,"
says Matthew.   But the second of the four Evangelists, with those wonderful eyes of his, says a still
more startling thing.   " He *began* to be *sore amazed* "
is Mark's inexpressibly striking contribution to this
awful, this absolutely unfathomable history.   Our
words, our very best words—even the words in
which the Holy Ghost teaches us—all fail us here.
The best and the most expressive of our words
do not come near describing our Lord in anything
He was, or in anything He did.   When our Lord
" *began* to be *sore amazed* and *very heavy*," it was

not such a beginning as ours even is. He began:
that is, He took a deliberate step : He performed
a deliberate act : He, of His own accord, opened
the doors of His soul : He poured in on His own
soul, He let pour, in all the unutterable woe of that
unutterably woeful night. We set ourselves, with
all our might, to see and to feel just what it was
that our Lord both did, and endured, that dreadful
night : but we give up the effort utterly baffled.
" It is too high, and we cannot attain to it." We
cannot wade out into all the waves of woe that went
over His soul that night and that morning. We
need not try it—for we cannot do it. He trod the
wine-press alone ; and of the people there was none
with Him. We should need to be both God and
man, as He was : we should need to be the Lamb of
God, as He was : we should need to be " made sin,"
as He was—before we could possibly understand in
what way " He began to be sorrowful and very
heavy." The second Evangelist far surpasses all
the rest, and he far surpasses himself, in his extraordinarily bold and soul-piercing word—" He began
to be *sore amazed*." Luther declared that, to him,
these words of Mark about our Lord were the most
astonishing words in the whole Bible. And that
saying of Luther's is to me a sure measure of the
greatness and the freshness of the Reformer's mind
and heart. Speaking for myself,—I have not come
on any word in the Bible that has more both in-

vited and then utterly baffled me to bottom than
just this word "amazed." I cannot *see* my Lord's
human soul as I here seem to be invited in to see it.
I cannot picture to my mind His experience at that
supreme moment. What was it that so "amazed"
our Lord in the Garden of Gethsemane? What was
there that could begin to so sore amaze Him to
whom all things were naked and open? There
was nothing that could so sore amaze the Son of
God, but only one thing. And that one thing was
sin. It was *sin* "laid upon Himself" till He was
"made *sin*." Sin is so unspeakably evil, and so
unspeakably awful in its evil, that it "sore amazed,"
and struck down, as to death and hell, the very
Son of God Himself. He had been "amazed"
enough at sin before now. He had seen sin making
angels of heaven into devils of hell. And He had
seen sin making men, made in the image of God,
to be the prey and the spoil, and the dwelling-places,
and the companions, of devils. He had seen and
He had studied all His days the whole malice and
wickedness of the heart of man. It had been amazement and horror enough to stand and see deceit
and envy and pride, and all of that kind, as He
describes it in terrible words, "coming out of the
heart" of man. But it was a new thing to our
Lord to have all that poured in upon Himself. To
be *made sin* "amazed" our Lord; it absolutely
overwhelmed Him,—cast Him into "an agony":

it loaded Him and sickened Him, and slew Him, down to death and hell. A terror at sin and a horror : a terror and a horror at Himself—to abso-· lute stupefaction—took possession of our Lord's soul when He was *made sin*. The only thing any- where at all like His amazement and heaviness, and exceeding sorrow and anguish, is the amaze- ment and the heaviness, and exceeding sorrow and utter anguish of God's saints ; when, in their life of highest holiness and most heavenly service, they, at the same time, both see and feel that they are still "made of sin," as Andrewes has it. Their utter stupefaction of soul as they see all hell opening and pouring up its bottomless wickedness all over their soul,—that is to taste something of what is behind of the " amazement " of Christ. That is to drink of His cup : that is to be baptized with His baptism. It was SIN, and it was sin *on* and *in* Himself,—it was pure and simple SIN that so amazed and agonised our Lord. Take away all its terrible wages : take away its sure and full discovery and exposure : take away its dreadful remorse : take away both the first and the second death : take away the day of judgment and the fire that is not quenched,—all which is the mere froth of the cup,—take away all that, and leave pure SIN : leave pure, essential, unadulterated SIN,—what the apostle so master- fully calls " the sinfulness of sin." Conceive *that*, if you have the imagination. Look at *that*, if your eyes have been sufficiently anointed. Taste *that*, if your tongue is sufficiently tender and strong. Carry about *that*, continually, in a broken, prayerful, holy heart—and you, of all men, are within a stone's-cast of Christ in the garden : you are too near, indeed, for mortal man to endure it long : if you remain long there you will need an angel from heaven to strengthen you.

It was not His approaching *death*. Death and all its terrors did not much move, did not much disconcert, did not much discompose our Lord. He went up to meet His death with a calmness and with a peacefulness of mind, with a stateliness and with a serenity of soul that confounded the Roman centurion, and almost converted the Governor himself. No. It was not death : it was SIN. It was that in which our mother conceived us : it was that which we drink up like water. It was that which we are full of, from the sole of the foot even to the head. It was that which never cost us an hour's sleep. It was that which never caused us— it may be—a single moment of pain, or shame, or amazement of soul. It was SIN. It was hell-fire in His soul. It was the coals, and the oil, and the rosin, and the juniper, and the turpentine of the fire that is not quenched. " The sorrows of death compassed me, and the pains of hell gat hold upon me. I found trouble and sorrow."

" We know that the law is spiritual : but I am

carnal, sold under sin. For that which I do I
allow not : for what I would, that do I not ; but
what I hate, that do I. . . . I find then a law, that,
when I would do good, evil is present with me. . . .
Oh, wretched man that I am! Who shall deliver
me from the body of this death ? . . . For the
flesh lusteth against the Spirit, and the Spirit against
the flesh : and these are contrary the one to the
other." *That* was not our Lord's amazement
and agony : but that is as near our Lord's
amazement and agony as any sinner can ever
come. Are you able to drink of My cup, and to be
baptized with My baptism ?—Christ says to every
true disciple of His, as He leads him down into the
Gethsemane of his sanctification. Till, as his true
sanctification—so very heavy, so exceeding sorrowful, so sore amazing—goes on, that man of God
enters into the " fellowship of the sufferings of
Christ "; to a depth of pain and shame and tears
and blood, that has to be hid away with Christ
among the wine-presses and the crosses and the
graves of the garden. For he—this elect soul—
wrestles not any more with flesh and blood, but
with principalities, and with powers, and with
spiritual wickednesses, in the high places of his own
soul.

" Who is this that cometh from Edom, with
dyed garments from Bozrah ? . . . Wherefore art
thou red in thine apparel, and thy garments like

him that treadeth in the wine-fat ? " The hollow of Jacob's thigh was out of joint as he wrestled with the angel. But with all that, there is one here greater than our father Jacob. Jacob halted on his thigh indeed, as he passed over Peniel. But our Lord's sweat with *His* agony was, as it were, great drops of blood falling to the ground. When the light of their lanterns shone on the dyed garments of the betrayed Man, who came to meet them, the Roman soldiers fell back. They had never before bound such a prisoner as that. There is no sword-stroke that they can see upon Him ; and yet His hands and His head and His beard are all full of blood. What a coat was that for which the soldiers cast their lots ! It was without seam, but,—all the nitre and soap they could wash it with,—the blood of the garden and of the pillar was so marked upon it, that it would not come out of it. What became, I wonder, of that " dyed " garment ? and all that " red apparel " ?

> If you have tears, prepare to shed them now.
> You all do know this mantle : I remember
> The first time Cæsar ever put it on ;
> 'Twas on a summer evening, in his tent,
> That day he overcame the Nervii :—
> Look, in this place ran Cassius' dagger through ;
> See what a rent the envious Casca made ;
> Through this the well-beloved Brutus stabbed ;
> And, as he plucked his cursed steel away,
> Mark, how the blood of Cæsar followed it, . . .
>   Then burst his mighty heart ;
> And, in his mantle muffling up his face,—

Even at the base of Pompey's statue,
Which all the while ran blood—great Cæsar fell.
O, what a fall was there, my countrymen ! . . .
Now let it work.

And as Peter preached on the day of Pentecost,
he lifted up the seamless robe he knew so well :
and, spreading it out in all its rents and all its blood-
spots, he charged his hearers, and said : " Him ye
have taken, and by wicked hands have crucified
and slain. . . . Therefore let all the house of Israel
know assuredly that God hath made that same
Jesus, whom ye have crucified, both Lord and
Christ."

" O piteous spectacle ! O noble Cæsar ! O
woeful day ! O most bloody sight ! Most noble
Cæsar, we'll revenge His death ! O royal Cæsar !
Here was a Cæsar ! When comes such another ?
Now let it work ! "

And, one way it will surely work is this,—to teach
us to pray, as He prayed. " And it came to pass,
that, as He was praying in a certain place,"—most
probably Gethsemane,—" when He ceased, one of
His disciples said unto Him, Lord, teach us to
pray ! "

1. Our blessed Lord had " a *place* " of prayer
that He was wont to retire to, till even Judas knew
the place. We should have said that the Son of
God did not need retirement and seclusion and
secrecy in order to seek and find His Father. We
should have said that He did not need our aids, and

instruments, and appliances, and means of grace. He was always "in the spirit." He was always collected, and disposed, and heavenly-minded. And yet, for reasons of His own, our Lord had a closed-in place of His own,—an olive-tree, a wine-press, a stone's-cast out of sight, where He sought and found His Father.

2. The wrestlers in the ancient lists went and practised themselves on the spot where they were to-morrow to close with their enemy. They went down into the arena alone. They looked around. They looked up at the seats where the spectators would sit. They looked up at the throne in which Cæsar would sit. They looked well at the iron door at which their enemy would come in. They felt their flesh. They exercised their joints. They threw, and were thrown, in imagination. And the victory was won before the day of their agony came. Pray much beside and upon your bed, my brethren. You will die, as you hope, in your bed. Well, make it, and yourself, ready. "Forefancy" the last enemy. Have your harness in repair. Feel the edge of your sword. Aye; cross the Kedron sometimes, and stand beside your fast-opening grave, and read your name on the cold stone. For,

The arrow seen beforehand slacks its flight.

3. And our last lesson is this : *Non multa, sed multum*, that is to say, "One thing is needful."

The cup! the cup! the cup! Our Lord did not
use many words: but He used His few words
again and again, till, *this cup*! and *Thy will*!—
Thy will be done, and this cup—was all His prayer.
Cato the Censor,—it did not matter what he was
speaking about in the Senate house, or what bill
was upon the table—ended every speech of his
with the same gesture, and with the same defiant
exclamation,—*Delenda est Carthago*! "The cup!"
"The cup!" "The cup!" cried Christ: first on
His feet: and then on His knees: and then on His
face. "Avenge me of mine adversary!" cried the
widow. "Avenge me of mine adversary! Avenge
me of mine adversary!" And, O God! this day,
from this day forward, avenge us of ours! Our one
and only enemy is sin. *Delenda,* avenge!

Lord, teach us to pray.

Now let it work!

XII

ONE OF PAUL'S PRAYERS

" Lord, teach us to pray."—LUKE xi. 1.
" For this cause I bow my knees unto the Father . . ."—
EPH. iii. 14-19.

IF we do not learn to pray, it will not be for want
of instructions and examples. Look at Abraham,
taking it upon him to speak unto the Lord for
Sodom. Look at Isaac, who goes out to meditate
in the field at the eventide. Look at Jacob, as
he wrestles until the breaking of the day at the
Jabbok. Look at Hannah, as she speaks in her
heart. Look at David, as he prevents now the
dawning of the day, and now the watches of the
night, in a hundred psalms. Look at our Lord.
And then, look at Paul, as great in prayer as he
is in preaching, or in writing Epistles. No,—if
you never learn to pray, it will not be for want of
the clearest instructions, and the most shining
examples.

Our Lord's Intercessory Prayer is above us : it
is beyond us. Of the people there are none with
our Lord when He prays. There is inexhaustible
instruction in our Lord's Intercessory Prayer ; but

we must take our examples from men like ourselves. After our Lord, there is no nobler sight to be seen on earth than Paul on his knees in his prison in Rome. All the Apostle's bonds fall from off him as he kneels in prayer for the saints in Ephesus, and for all the faithful in Christ Jesus. Truly the Apostle has not fainted in his tribulations when he can rise to such intercession and adoration as this. "For this cause I bow my knees unto the Father of our Lord Jesus Christ, of whom the whole family in heaven and earth is named."

> Stone walls do not a prison make,
> Nor iron bars a cage !

No,—not when those stone walls and those iron bars have an Apostle Paul within them. For, as Paul kneels on his prison floor, its dark roof becomes a canopy of light : and its walls of iron become crystal till Paul sees the whole family in heaven and on earth gathered together in one, and all filled with the fulness of God. Not Jews and Gentiles only, of twain made one new man ; but all created things that are in heaven, and that are in earth, visible and invisible, whether they be thrones, or dominions, or principalities, or powers. He sees all the angels of God in all their endless ministries. He sees the Archangels in their mighty dominions. He sees the Cherubim shining with knowledge, and the Seraphim burning with love. "Every family,"

is Paul's great and all-embracing word, "every
family in heaven and earth." Paul sees them all;
he salutes them all: he loves them all: he prays
for them all. Paul has the heart of a brother toward
them all. And all that, because his Father is their
Father; and his God their God; and his Master their
Master. And as he looks up at them with wonder,
they look down at him with desire. Much as they
could tell him, they feel that he could tell them
far more. They are not ignorant of God: God
hath not left His heavenly families without a
witness. Both in their creation and in their con-
firmation; both in their occupations and in their
wages; both in their worship and in their wars,—
they all live, and move, and have their being in
God. But some of their elect and travelled fellows
have returned, and have told them things that
have set all their hearts on fire. Gabriel, for one;
the angel who was sent with strength to the Garden
of Gethsemane, for another; as also the multitude
of the heavenly host who praised God and said,
" Glory to God in the highest ! "—all these favoured
sons of God had it to tell their fellows that not
the seventh heaven itself, but this lowest earth
alone, had seen the fulness of the Father's love.
And not in envy but in love they " desire to look
into these things." Paul from his prison looks
up to them, and they from a thousand shining
walls and towers and battlements and palaces look

down at him. And then, both earth and heaven
simultaneously cease from one another, and look
at Christ. " And the number of them was ten
thousand times ten thousand, and thousands of
thousands ; saying with a loud voice, Blessing and
honour and glory and power : Amen ! " And as
the angels sang, Paul rose up off his knees, and took
his pen and wrote this to us : " For verily He took
not on Him the nature of angels : but He took on
Him the seed of Abraham. . . . Wherefore, holy
brethren, partakers of the heavenly calling, consider
the Apostle and High Priest of our profession,
Christ Jesus "

Let us then also, my brethren, as often as
we lift our eyes and look up at the sun and
the moon and the stars,—at Arcturus, and the
bands of Orion, and the sweet influences of Pleiades,
and the Chambers of the South—let us see, inhabit-
ing and holding them all for God, His " every
family " named after Him. Let us often visit in
faith, and in love, and in imagination, all the
Father's families, intellectual and moral and
spiritual, that people the whole created universe.
Let us lift up our hands and salute them, and love
them in God their Maker, and in Jesus Christ their
Strength, if not also their Redeemer. If they are
not jealous of us, we need not be jealous of the
best of them. As yet they far excel us in glory :
but they would count it all loss to be " found in

Christ not having their own righteousness." Yes :
come, all ye shining angels of God, and I will tell
you what He hath done for my soul! Tell me
about your God, and I will tell you about my God.
How has He made you ? And out of what substance ? And just in what image ? How has He
spoken and written to you, and in what language
of Heaven ? In what way has the *Logos* enlightened
you ? In what way has the Son, Who is in the
bosom of the Father, revealed the Father to you ?
Just in what way do you know what is to be known
of God ? Is there no kind of sin among you ?
Did you ever hear about sin ? Do you know what
it is ? When one of your number is talented, and
favoured, and employed, and trusted, and loved,
and brought nearer the throne than another, what
do you feel to your brother in your hearts ? Do
your hearts grow richer in love as your ages go on ?
Or have you ages in Heaven ? Have you days and
nights and weeks and years in Heaven ? Do you
never grow old ? Have you no death ? What is
your occupation ? What are your wages ? What
is your way of taking rest ? How do you worship ?
How much do you know about us ? Can you see
us at your distance ? Has anyone of our race of
men ever visited your cities ? And what did he
tell you about himself, and about us ? Oh, all ye
lofty worlds of life, and light, and obedience, and
blessedness, we take boldness to salute you in

the name of our Father,—in His great Name, after
which every family in heaven and earth is named !

Far more out of the body than in it, the Apostle
now bows his knees to the Father for that little
family of saints and faithful in Christ Jesus that
God has in Ephesus, " that He would grant them
to be strengthened with might by His spirit in the
inner man." What a sweep of spiritual vision
from every family in heaven down to the inner
man of every Ephesian believer ! What wonderful
flights of spiritual vision Paul took ! And with
what swiftness and sureness of wing ! But, what
exactly is this that he here prays for with such
importunity and nobility of mind ? What is the
" inner man " ? And what is the strength of the
inner man ? An illustration is far better than a
description. And our Lord Himself—Blessed be
His Name !—is the best description and illustration
of spiritual strength in the inner man. " And the
child grew," we read, " and waxed strong in spirit,
filled with wisdom, and the Grace of God was upon
Him." Was upon Him, and was within Him, till
He stood up in the fulness of that wisdom and that
strength, and took the Book, and found the place,
and said to the men among whom He had been
brought up, " This day is this Scripture fulfilled in
your ears." And, from that notable day, our Lord's
whole life was one long and unbroken illustration
to us of that strength in the inner man that

we are now in search of. When He loved His enemies : when He did good to them that hated Him : when He blessed them that cursed Him : when He prayed for them that despitefully used Him : when, smitten on the one cheek, He offered also the other : when His cloke was taken away, and He forbade them not to take His coat also : when He gave to him that asked of Him : when He did to all men as He would have all men do to Him : when He judged not, nor found fault, but forgave as much as if He had Himself needed to be forgiven : when He was merciful, even as His Father in Heaven is merciful : when He gave, looking not to receive again, good measure, pressed down, shaken together, and running over into men's bosoms : " when He was reviled, and reviled not again : when He suffered and threatened not . . . but His own self bare our sins in His own body on the tree "—that was strength in the inner man. Paul, himself, in no small measure, had in himself the same inner man and the strength that his Master had. " For this thing I besought the Lord thrice, that it might depart from me. And He said unto me, My grace is sufficient for thee : for My strength is made perfect in weakness. . . . Therefore I take pleasure in infirmities, in reproaches, in necessities, in persecutions, in distresses for Christ's sake : for when I am weak, then am I strong."

Now, were some true and Paul-like friend of ours,
who has power with God, to bow his knees to the
Father for this same strength to strengthen us in
our inner man—how would the answer show itself?
It would show itself in this way. In that thing in
which we are now so weak, so easily tempted, so
easily overtaken, and so easily overthrown—in that
thing, and at that time, we should then stand firm.
At what times and in what places in your life do
you bring shame and pain and defeat and bondage
on yourselves? In what are you a burden, and an
offence, and a hindrance, and a constant cross to
your families and friends and acquaintances? Well,
all that would then come to an end, or, if not all at
once to an end,—as it would not,—yet all that would
begin to come to an end. With that strength
strengthening you in the inner man, you would begin
to be patient and silent and strong to endure under
provocation. You would be able to command
yourself where you were wont to be lashed up into
a passion. You would begin to look on the things
of other men. You would enjoy other men's happiness as, at present, you enjoy your own. You
would be as grieved to hear an evil report of other
men as it to-day kills you to be told evil reports
about yourself. You would rejoice with them that
do rejoice: and you would weep with them who
weep. You would suffer long, and you would be
kind: you would not entertain envy: you would

not vaunt yourself : you would not be puffed up :
you would not behave yourself unseemly : you
would not seek your own : you would not be easily
provoked ; you would think no evil : you would not
rejoice in iniquity, but you would rejoice in the
truth : you would bear all things, believe all
things, hope all things, endure all things. In
all these things, as the outward man perished,
the inward man would be renewed day by day.
Brethren, pray for us ! And God forbid that we
should sin against the Lord in ceasing to pray
for you !

But the interceding Apostle contracts and concentrates this prayer of his for the Ephesians in a
very remarkable way. He concentrates and directs
his prayer on one special kind of strength. Paul is
as much bent on finding faith in the Ephesians as
Christ was bent on finding it in Jew and in Gentile,
and was overjoyed when He found it. " That
Christ may dwell in your hearts by faith." But
how ?—just in what way does Christ dwell in that
man's heart in which faith is strengthened ? Well,
take an illustration again. How did the still absent
bridegroom dwell in the heart of the bride in the
song ? Listen to her heart, and you will see for
yourself. "By night on my bed I sought him
whom my soul loveth : I sought him, but I found
him not. Saw ye him whom my soul loveth ? I
charge you, O daughters of Jerusalem, that ye tell

him that I am sick of love. Oh, that thou wert as my
brother, that sucked the breasts of my mother !
I would lead thee, and bring thee into my mother's
house. His left hand should be under my head,
and his right hand should embrace me. Set me
as a seal upon thine heart, as a seal upon thine arm :
for love is strong as death. Many waters cannot
quench love, neither can the floods drown it."
That is something of the way Christ dwells in his
heart who is strengthened by faith. That is the way
he dwelt in John and Paul and in our own Samuel
Rutherford. And why not in you and me ? Simply
because no one has prayed for us, and we have not
prayed for ourselves, that Christ may dwell in our
hearts by faith. No prayer,—no faith,—no Christ in
the heart. Little prayer,—little faith,—little Christ
in the heart. Increasing prayer,—increasing faith,—
increasing Christ in the heart. Much prayer,—much
faith,—much Christ in the heart. Praying always,—
faith always,—Christ always. " Hitherto ye have
asked nothing in My name : ask, and ye shall receive,
that your joy may be full."

" That ye, being rooted and grounded in love,
may be able to comprehend with all saints what is
the breadth, and length, and depth, and height ;
and to know the love of Christ, which passeth
knowledge." You cannot construe that. You
cannot make grammar and logic out of that. You
cannot make theological science out of that. You

cannot shut that up into a confession of faith, or
contract it into a Church catechism. Paul is a
mystic. Paul is a poet. Paul is of heart and
imagination all compact. Paul has science, and he
has clearness and crispness of intellect of the very
first order. But he will tell you himself that he
never in any of his Epistles speaks the words which
man's wisdom teacheth, but which the Holy Ghost
teacheth, because they are spiritually discerned.
" Rooted and grounded." I defy you when you
first try it to make anything of that. I defy you,
all you can do, to reconcile that. You never saw
anything like that in all your experience. There
is nothing created by God, or manufactured by
man, like that. You never heard before this
prayer, nor have you ever heard since this prayer,
of anything that was both rooted and grounded.
There is no such thing. There is no such thing but
a saint's heart. A tree is rooted, and a house is
grounded : a tree has a root, and a house has a
foundation : but no house has a root, and no tree
has a foundation. No houses but holy hearts : no
trees but the trees of righteousness, the planting of
the Lord. But here—all you who love to hear of
wonders and strange tales—here is a house with
roots, and a tree with foundations ! And all that
deep down in the divine ground of love. Magnificent man ! A master of men ! A master of the
inner man of the heart ! Great Paul ! Great

original ! Great Apostle ! Both Apostle and Poet of Jesus Christ !

" And to know the love of Christ, which passeth knowledge." There, again ! What can we make of a man like Paul ? You cannot draw out leviathan with a hook. Wilt thou play with him as with a bird ? Or wilt thou bind him for thy maidens ? He maketh the sea to shine after him. One would think the deep to be hoary. And yet, do not despair ! For it is this same leviathan among men who has written with his own hand this combined challenge and encouragement. " Where is the wise ? Where is the scribe ? Where is the disputer of this world ? Because the foolishness of God is wiser than men. . . . That your faith should not stand in the wisdom of men, but in the power of God." Yes ! I begin to see ! It passes knowledge to know it all : but, if it were not possible to me to know the love of Christ in my own measure, Paul would never mock me by such a prayer. All saints, he says, know that love well. Then the least saint, and he who is not worthy to be called a saint, may have his own little knowledge of that love. A saint, indeed, is not a saint at all : a true saint is just a great sinner seeking to taste the love of Christ. Only " tell me which of them will love Him most . . . I suppose He to whom He forgave most . . . Thou has rightly judged."

The truth, my brethren, the blessed truth is

this—that instead of it being a difficulty, and a
hardship, and an offence that the love of Christ
passeth knowledge,—that is the crowning glory of
Christ's love : that is our crowning blessedness.
The love of Christ has no border : it has no shore :
it has no bottom. The love of Christ is boundless :
it is bottomless : it is infinite : it is divine. That it
passeth knowledge is the greatest thing that ever
was said, or could be said about it, and Paul was
raised up of all men to see that and to say it. We
shall come to the shore, we shall strike the bottom, of
every other love : but never of the love of Christ !
No, never ! It passeth now, and it will for ever
pass, knowledge. You, who have once cast yourselves into it, and upon it—the great mystic speaks
of it as if it were at once an ocean and a mountain,
—you will never come to the length of it, or to the
breadth of it, or to the depth of it, or to the height
of it. To all eternity, the love of Christ to you
will be new. It will fill you full of wonder, and
expectation, and imagination ; full of joy and
sweetness and satisfaction : and still the half
will not be known to you. Heap up eternity
upon eternity, and still the love of Christ to
you will make all eternity to be but the spring-
time of life to you, and still but the early
days of your everlasting espousals. The love of
Christ will, absolutely and everlastingly, pass
all knowledge. The love of Christ, like the

peace of God, will everlastingly pass all understanding.

" And, that ye might be filled with all the fulness
of God." What that is, and what that will for ever
be,—" it is not lawful for a man to utter."

XIII

ONE OF PAUL'S THANKSGIVINGS

"Lord, teach us to pray."—Luke xi. 1.
"Giving thanks unto the Father . . ."—Col. i. 12, 13.

THANKSGIVING is a species of prayer. Thanksgiving is one species of prayer out of many. Prayer, in its whole extent and compass, is a comprehensive and compendious name for all kinds of approach and all kinds of address to God, and for all kinds and all degrees of communion with God. Request, petition, supplication; acknowledgment and thanksgiving; meditation and contemplation; as, also, all our acts and engagements of public, and family, and closet worship,—all those things are all so many species, so to say, of prayer. Petition is the lowest, the most rudimentary and the most elementary of all kinds of prayer. And it is because we so seldom rise above the rudiments and first principles of divine things that we so seldom think, and so seldom speak, about prayer in any other sense than in that of request and petition and supplication. Whereas praise—pure, emancipated, enraptured, adoring praise,—is the supremest and the most perfect of all kinds of prayer. Thanksgiving is

higher and purer than petition ; while, again, it is
lower and less blessed than holy, heavenly, God-
adoring praise.

Now it is to thanksgiving that the Apostle
here invites the Colossian believers. He has
prayed for them ever since the day on which he first
heard of their faith and their love. And now,
that Epaphras has brought him such good news
of their continuance and their growth in grace, he
invites them to join with him in this noble thanksgiving—unto the Father who hath delivered him
and them from the power of darkness and hath
translated him and them into the Kingdom of His
dear Son.

It is in Paul's princely manner to establish and
to illustrate his doctrines, and to enforce and to fix
his counsels, by drawing upon his own experience.
This is one of Paul's great ways of writing, and it is
only a true and a great man who could write about
himself as Paul constantly writes. Paul is so dead
in Paul that he can take an argument, and a proof,
and an illustration, and an apostrophe out of himself
with as much liberty and detachment as if he had
lived in the days of Moses or of David. Paul is so
" crucified with Christ " that he can speak about
himself, on occasion, as if he were speaking about
some other man altogether. " I knew a man in
Christ, above fourteen years ago : whether in the
body, or out of the body, I cannot tell : God

knoweth." Speaking, then, out of this noble
freedom and self-emancipation, Paul puts himself
at the head of the Colossians in their thanksgiving
and says : Come, O ye saints and faithful brethren,
and join with me in my constant thanksgiving
to the Father, "Which hath made us meet to be
partakers of the inheritance of the saints in light :
Who hath delivered us "—first me and then you
—" from the power of darkness, and hath translated
us into the kingdom of His dear Son." "Us," he
says,—you and me. And especially me, that I
might be a pattern to them which should hereafter
believe on Him to life everlasting.

"Darkness" and "the power of darkness."
Now, what is this darkness ? It is sin, you will
answer. And so it is. It is sin. It is the dark
shadow that sin casts on God and on the soul of
the sinner. This is not what we are wont to call
"darkness." This is not the slow setting, or the
sudden eclipse, of the sun or the moon. This is not
the overclouding of the stars. This is not the oil
failing till our lamps go out. This is not the darkness that terrifies our children. This is not the
darkness that is scattered by striking a match and
lighting a candle. No. This "darkness" is sin.
And each man's own, and only, darkness is from
his own sin. And each man's darkness is so thick,
and so inward, and so abiding, because it is the
darkness that is cast by that huge idol of darkness,

each man's own sinful self. "Self," in this life, is just another, and a truer, and a keener, and a more homecoming name, for sin. My sin is myself. And my darkness lies so thick and so deadly on my soul because self towers up so high and so dark in my soul. And in every man's soul! That is the reason that the world is so full of all kinds of darkness,—because it is so full of men who are all so full of themselves. And that is the reason that hell is so full of darkness,—with not one ray of light,—it is because it is so full of fallen angels and fallen men who are all so full of themselves. That is the reason why they gnaw their tongues with pain, and that is the reason that the smoke of their torment goes up for ever. Yes : believe it ! yes : be sure of it ! Self is the very valley of the shadow of death. It is the land of deserts and pits. It is that land of drought through which no man passes. It is that land where all men who pass through it stumble and are broken upon its dark mountains. Hell is hell, because self fills it full, down and out, to all its awful bottomlessness. And heaven is heaven, because there is no self there. Only God is there : only the Father, and the Son, and the Holy Ghost, and our neighbour as ourselves. And self in Paul, and in the Colossians, was hell begun : it was hell and its darkness in them already; till the Father gave commandment and delivered them from this darkness of sin and self, and translated them into the marvellous light of His dear Son.

Paul is a magnificent writer. We have seen one magnificent manner of Paul's writing already ; and there is another in this magnificent passage. But both these manners of his are too high, and too much his own, for any of us to attain to, or to attempt. We must not measure common men with the measure of the Apostle Paul. After he had been caught up into Paradise, Paul never altogether got himself brought back to this earth again. His conversation and his correspondence ever after that was carried on in " unspeakable words." His affection, ever after that, was set on things above, and not on things on the earth. He wrote all his Epistles, after that, less in any language that has ever been written on earth than in the language they write and speak and sing in heaven. His very pen and ink and parchment after that, his very grammar and vocabulary, his style, —his whole intellectual and moral and spiritual manner,—no school on earth ever taught this Apostle to write these Epistles. He writes in the mood, in the tense, in the idiom, in the atmosphere, in the scope, and in the horizon of heaven. Time and sin are already no longer with Paul, when he is at his best. Paul sits in heavenly places with Christ, and he writes to us in words it is not lawful for a man to utter. And he is so assured con-

cerning not himself only but concerning all the
chosen and called in Christ Jesus, that he antedates
his Epistles, and writes in them, as if all the
Colossians and Ephesians and Thessalonians were
already where he is. He sometimes redresses the
balance in a most masterly manner ; but his prevailing tone and temper is that of a glorified saint,
who both sees and experiences what other saints
still but believe in and hope for. " The Father
hath delivered us," says Paul ecstatically, where a
less rapt and a more pedestrian writer would be
thankful to be able to say : He has begun to deliver
us, and it is our unceasing prayer that He will
perfect that which so concerneth us ! I do not ask
you, my brethren, to be thankful like Paul and the
Colossians, because the Father has actually and for
ever delivered you from the darkness of selfishness,
and anger, and envy, and malice, and lovelessness,
and unbelief, and all disobedience. I dare not ask
you to be thankful for your deliverance as if it
were perfected and past. For, if I said you had
no sin, I should be a liar. And if I said you were
delivered from all darkness, you would laugh in my
face and say I was a fool. All I ask is this—Do you
know what Paul is speaking about ? Do you have
this darkness of his in yourself ? Is there less of it
than there once was ? Do you hate the darkness,
and yourself on account of it ? and do you rejoice
in the light and seek it ? Are your dark thoughts

about your neighbour your daily burden and
agonising prayer ? Do you, before God, put off
the deeds and the words and the thoughts of darkness, and put on against them the armour of light ?
Do you, my brethren, do you ?   Then Paul, hearing
of all that from Epaphras, would write an Epistle
to you in his most soaring style, till you would
answer : "Would God, He had indeed so delivered me ! " And he would answer you back
again, and would say, " When Christ, Who is our
life, shall appear, then shall ye also appear with
Him in glory. Put on, therefore, as the elect of
God, holy and beloved, bowels of mercies, kindness,
humbleness of mind, meekness, long-suffering ;
forbearing one another, and forgiving one another,
if any man have a quarrel against any " : and in all
that the Father will more and more deliver you
from the power of darkness, and will "translate
you into the kingdom of His dear Son."

" He delivered us " is tame and jejune.   " He
snatched us," is Paul's tingling and heart-thrill-
ing word. He snatched us as the angel snatched
Lot out of Sodom ! He snatched us as a man
snatches a brand out of the fire.   " And while
Lot lingered, the men laid hold upon his hand,
and upon the hand of his wife, and upon the
hand of his two daughters ; the Lord being
merciful unto him : and they brought him forth,
and set him without the city."   And like that,—

yes, often like that,—when a darkness is again,
as of Sodom and Gomorrah, filling our hearts,
God takes our hand, and we are in repentance,
and in prayer, and in tears, and in love to God
and man, before we know where we are. " The
sun was risen upon the earth when Lot entered
into Zoar."

He " snatched " us and translated us : literally,
He emigrated us. Now an emigrant is more than
a delivered captive. An emigrant, even when you
emigrate him, goes of his own free will and full
accord. He chooses to go. He decides to go. He
prepares to go. He hastens to go. You tell him
about a better land. You fit him out for it. You
even pay his passage to it, and buy him his farm in
it : but all that only makes him the more forward
to go to it. "Come ! " he says to his wife and
children, " let us be up and going ! " And so is
it with those whom the Father emigrates. They
have far more hand in their translation and emigra-
tion into the Kingdom of God's dear Son than they
had in their snatched deliverance from the power of
darkness. They love the light now. They love
to hear about it. They love to walk in it.   " Every
one that doeth evil hateth the light, neither
cometh to the light, lest his deeds should be reproved. But he that doeth truth cometh to the
light, that his deeds may be made manifest, that
they are wrought in God."

And, lastly, in this great thanksgiving : He hath " made us meet to be partakers of the inheritance of the saints in light."

" Meet " is a fine translation, and an exquisitely apt and beautiful English expression—as long as our minds move only in the literature of the text. But when we take the text to heart, it runs through our hearts like a two-edged sword. O Paul ! up in Paradise, be merciful in thy rapture ! Hast thou forgotten that thou, also, wast once a wretched man ? " Darkness " I know. And " Deliverance from the power of darkness " I am not altogether ignorant of. God's dear Son and His Kingdom,—I sometimes feel as if I had indeed been " translated " into it. But, " meet for the inheritance of the saints in light ! " My heart is dazzled and driven back, and driven down within me, with the too great glory. *I* meet for that inheritance ! Impossible, for I am to this day full of darkness and of everything that is *un*meet for such an inheritance ! I was saying that to myself, my brethren, over this Scripture, when a voice spake to me and said : " What do you say to the thief on the cross ? " At first I did not see what the thief on the cross had to do with my hopeless *un*meetness for the heavenly inheritance. But, gradually, there arose in my mind what the thief asked of the Dying Redeemer, and what the Dying Redeemer promised the thief. Hanging by his hands and his feet, and

filled with the darkness of a lifetime of robbery
and murder, the near neighbourhood of the Saviour
for those six hours made such an impression on the
dying thief that the whole impossible work of the
text was gathered up, and completed, in that great
sinner that forenoon. " Lord, remember me when
Thou comest into Thy Kingdom." . . . " To-day
shalt thou be with Me in Paradise." That thief
then, who, by his own confession, was only reaping
on the cross as he had sown all his days—that thief
was in Paradise before Paul himself : Paul saw
him, and talked with him : and he must have been
made as *meet* for Paradise as Paul himself. In
those six hours of pain, and shame, and repentance,
and sight of Christ beside him in His sweetness, and
meekness, and patience, and pity and prayer for
His murderers—that forenoon, the Father delivered
that outcast creature, snatched him from the power
of darkness and translated him into the Kingdom of
His dear Son. And, more marvellous still, and past
all our understanding how it was done, He made
him meet, and that in a moment, for the inheritance
of the saints in light. As soon as I saw that, I
understood the voice that had said to me, " Go,
before you preach your sermon, go and stand and
hear what passes between your Master and the
penitent thief." And I came away with new hope
for all my dying people, and for myself, and for our
meetness for the inheritance of the saints in light.

Have I then, and have you, that dying thief's meetness ? Have our sins found us out to the cross ? Has the darkness of death got hold of us ? And is our lost life fast running out of us like his life's blood? And, with all that, has there been given us a glimpse of Jesus Christ,—Jesus Christ in His affability and grace, and such affability and grace, and He Himself on the Cross ? Do you see and feel anything of all that ? Then, that is the Father ! That is the darkness beginning to divide, and clear up and scatter. You are on the border of the Kingdom of His dear Son. Follow that out, speak that out, say, " Lord, remember me ! " Tell Him that you are reaping the reward of your deeds in all the darkness, and in all the forsakenness, and in all the pain, and in all the death that has come upon you.

> The dying thief rejoiced to see
> That fountain in his day ;
> And there have I, as vile as he,
> Washed all my sins away.
>
> Dear dying Lamb, Thy precious blood
> Shall never lose its power
> Till all the ransomed Church of God
> Be saved, to sin no more.

Tell Him what you would rather die than tell to any other. Tell Him that He only knows how un-meet you are for anything to be called an inheritance of saints. But boldly tell Him also where your heart is. Tell Him that your heart is in heaven :

and testify to Him that even if He casts you into
hell, to all eternity your heart will be with Him and
His saints in heaven.   And, when you are as near
death as that thief was, keep on saying · Lord,
remember me !   Give Him no rest till He says : By
your much coming you weary Me.   And till He
says : Be it unto thee as thou wilt.   To-day shalt
thou be with Me !

XIV

THE MAN WHO KNOCKED AT MIDNIGHT

"Lord, teach us to pray."—LUKE xi. 1.

"Which of you shall have a friend, and shall go unto him at midnight . . ."—LUKE xi. 5–8.

IT is night. It is midnight. The night is dark. All the lights are out, and everybody is in bed. "Friend! lend me three loaves! For a friend of mine in his journey is come to me, and I have nothing to set before him!" He knocks again. "Friend! lend me three loaves!" He waits awhile and then he knocks again. "Friend, friend! I must have three loaves!" "Trouble me not : the door is now shut ; I cannot rise and give thee!" He is dumb, for a time. He stands still. He turns to go home. But he cannot go home. He dare not go home. He comes back. He knocks again. "Friend!" he cries, till the dogs bark at him. He puts his ear to the door. There is a sound inside, and then the light of a candle shines through the hole of the door. The bars of the door are drawn back, and he gets not three loaves only but as many as he needs. "And I say

unto you, Ask, and it shall be given you ; seek, and
ye shall find ; knock, and it shall be opened unto
you."

1. Our Lord Himself was often like that importunate poor man, out at midnight, knocking for
bread.   When He was a child, He had lain, full
of fear, and had heard all that knocking at midnight at Joseph's door.   And, when He became a
man, He remembered that sleepless midnight, and
spiritualised it and put it into this parable.   And
often, when He was full of all manner of labours,
and all manner of temptations all day, He called to
mind that midnight in Nazareth, and knocked again
and again till He got as much as He needed.   There
are things in the Gospels written there—without
emotion and without exclamation—at which our
hearts stand still, when we suddenly come upon
them.   " He went up into a mountain to pray :
and when the evening was come He was there
alone."   And, again, " He departed again into
a mountain Himself alone."   And, again, " It came
to pass in those days that He went out into a
mountain to pray, and continued all night in prayer
to God."   He continued all night.   Do you see
Him ?   Do you hear Him ?   Can you make out
what He is asking ?   He stands up.   He kneels
down.   He falls on His face.   He knocks at the
thick darkness.   All that night He prays, and
refuses to faint, till the sun rises, and He descends to

His disciples like a strong man to run a race. And
in Gethsemane all His past experiences in prayer,
and all He had ever said to His disciples about
prayer,—all that came back to His mind till His
sweat was as it were great drops of blood falling
to the ground. No,—we have not an high priest
who cannot be touched with the feeling of our
infirmities. "Who in the days of His flesh, when He
had offered up prayers and supplications with strong
crying and tears . . . And being made perfect,
He became the author of eternal salvation unto all
them that obey Him." And in nothing more than
in importunate prayer.

2. And then, just as He was when He was
in this world, and just as this importunate
poor man was, so are we while the day of our
mercy lasts in this world. A friend of ours—
so to call him—comes to us in his journey ; and
we have nothing to set before him. God's law
comes and says to us, Do this, and do that to that
man, pointing him out to us. And we set out to
do what we are told from God to do : but the thing
that we would, we do not : while the thing that
we would not, that we do. A temptation that we
had not expected, and that we were not prepared
for, comes upon us. A heart-searching, a heart-
scorching temptation,—till our hearts are as dark
as midnight, and as dead as the grave. Duties
that we cannot perform as we ought, and cannot

escape, are laid upon us. Trials to test and to sift us; and crosses to which to nail our hands and our feet, till, all day, and every day, and every night, like the man in the parable, we have nothing to set before them.

And then, in our famine of life, and peace, and strength, we think—oh, so unwillingly!—of God. How unwelcome is the thought that He has all that we need; and that, if we ask it aright of Him, He will give us all we need! It may be so. But if we could make any other shift we would make it. We have grace enough left to be ashamed to go to God in our need. It is so long since we have been at His door, or in His house, or at His table, or He at ours. He might very well say to us, I do not know you. He might very well say to us, Get some of your own friends to help you. We anticipate that, and also far worse upbraidings than that. And we turn back, we simply cannot go to God. But the intolerable pangs go on. The awful faintness and sinking go on : till very death itself, and worse than death, is at the door, and till we say like the four lepers at the entering in of the gate of Samaria : " Why sit we here until we die ? Now, therefore, come and let us fall unto the host of the Syrians : if they save us alive, we shall live : and if they kill us, we shall but die." It is not a very becoming mind in which to arise and go to our Father. But any of you that is a father does not

stand upon points with his son, which was dead, and
is alive again ; and was lost, and is found.

3. When the Books are opened it will be discovered that more importunate and prevailing
prayer has been offered at *midnight* than at all the
other hours of the day and the night taken together.
Look back at your Bible,—that book of importunate
and prevailing prayer,—and see ! Jacob is the father
of all men of importunate prayer. Jacob was
called no more Jacob, but Israel, because of his
all-night importunity in prayer. A friend of his,
his brother Esau, indeed, was to meet him to-
morrow, and Jacob felt that he must have all night
with God if his life was to be preserved. The sin
of his youth had found Jacob out. And it took
Jacob all night to see the sin of his youth as God
saw it, and as Esau saw it. But he *did* see it as
the night went on. And he called the name of
the place Peniel. What midnights David had with
sin, and with prayer also, all his Psalms testify.
But, best of all, David's Son. The midnight
mountains and the midnight olive-yards of Galilee
and Judea will all rise against us when the Books
are opened,—the Books about our Lord's life of
prayer, and the books about our own life of prayer.
His Books are all closed against that day, but not
ours yet. If, to-night, then, a friend of yours
should come to you, and you have nothing to set
before him : if, in your Saviour's words, you should

come to yourself to-night : and, amid your fear, or your want, or whatever form your awakening may take, if you hear over you and within you this voice saying to you : " Ask, and it shall be given you : seek, and ye shall find : knock, and it shall be opened unto you " : then do it. Do it, as if the Books were to be opened before the world is awake to-morrow morning. Do it, as if already the thief were at your window. Keep your candle burning till you read once more the Parable of the Friend at Midnight. Go through the parable : and go through it on your knees, if not yet on your face. Read it ; see it. See Himself,—the Son of God,— praying in a certain place. Attend to Him as He teaches His disciples to pray. See the man at midnight. Imitate that man. Act it all alone at midnight. Leave nothing of it that you do not do over again. See him in his straits. Hear his knocks sounding in the silence of the night. Hear his loud cry, and cry it after him. He needed three loaves. What is your need ? Name it. Name it out. Let your own ears hear it. And should some ear in the house overhear it, it will do them good to hear that sound in your room at midnight. Never mind the lateness of the hour : think of the untimeous man in the parable : think of your untimeous Intercessor, and continue in importunate prayer.

4. " Importunity,"—" because of his impor-

tunity,"—does not do justice to our Lord's style,—
to call it style. What our Lord said was far more
to the purpose than "importunity," excellent as
that is. What He said was "shamelessness." This
was what our Lord really said: "I say unto you,"
He said, "though he will not rise and give him
because he is his friend, yet because of his shamelessness he will rise and give him as many as he
needeth." "Think shame!" the man cried out,
who was in bed, with his door shut. "Think
shame!" the disturbed neighbours cried out.
"Think shame!" the late passers-by said. "Hold
your peace," they said, "and let honest men's
doors alone at this time of night." "Never mind,"
says our Lord on the other hand. "Never you mind
them: they have bread enough at home: and easy
for them to cry shame to a starving man. Never
you mind, knock you on. I have been in your
place Myself, till they said that I was beside Myself.
Knock you on: and I will stand beside you till I
see the door open. He must rise if you go on
knocking. Give him no rest. Well done! Knock
again!" Yes,—shamelessness! "What a shame-
less wretch I am!" you will say about yourself,
"to ask such things, to have to ask such things at
my age: to knock so loud after the way I have
neglected prayer, and neglected and forgotten the
Hearer of prayer." "At my age,"—you will
number your days and will blush with shame,—

"at my age, and only beginning to pray in any
earnest ! How many nights have I had no time
to give to God ! And, now, to expect that when
I lift up my finger, and go down five minutes on
my carpeted knees, God Almighty is to hasten and
set everything aside to hear me ! " Yes: you are
right : it needs some forehead: it needs some
face : it needs, as Christ says, some "shamelessness " in you and me to come in that manner and
for these things at midnight. Yes,—it is this that
so increases and so aggravates the shamelessness
of your case. The shameful things you have to
ask for. The disgraceful—the incredible things
you have to admit and confess. The life you have
lived. The way you have spent your days and
nights. And what all that has brought you to.
It kills you to have to say such things even with
your door shut. Yes,—but better say all these
things in closets than have them all proclaimed
from the housetops of the day of judgment. Knock,
man ! knock for the love of God ! Knock as they
knock to get into heaven after the door is shut !
Knock, as they knock to get out of hell !

5. And then,—oh ! what an experience it is,
what a more than heavenly joy it is, when the door
is at last opened, and the loaves are handed out !
What an indescribable feeling is that in our hearts,
when, after years of prayer, followed with midnight
after midnight of importunity and agony, light

begins to break through : and God's hand is reached out, and our souls taste the strength and the sweetness of the Bread from heaven. Jacob does not feel his thigh any more. David's couch, wet with his tears, is all answered now. The bloody sweat of Gethsemane itself is all forgotten now.

6. And, then, just before He shuts up His sermon on prayer, our Lord in one word touches the top and the perfection of all prayer, — importunate prayer, that is, for *the Holy Spirit*. It is no longer a prayer for bread, or for a fish, or for an egg : it is no longer for long life, or for riches, or for the life of our enemies : it. is no longer, What shall we eat ? or what shall we drink ? or wherewithal shall we be clothed ? It is now for the Holy Spirit, and for the Holy Spirit alone. Our Lord would fain hear us saying at the end of His sermon : " One thing do I desire, and that will I seek after." We have all wrestled at midnight, when we saw Esau coming to meet us with his armed men. We have all made our couch to swim with tears when our sin found us out. We have all fallen on our face when death, with his cords and his torches and his weapons, was seen crossing the Kedron. But have we ever been like this man in the parable for the Holy Spirit ? For the Holy Spirit, and for His holiness in our hearts ? Do we ever—do we often —do we without ceasing knock for holiness ? For the death and the destruction of sin in our souls ?

For faith in God,—to believe that He is when we
come to Him ?   For love to Jesus Christ ?   For
love to our neighbour ?   For love to our false
friends ? and to our enemies ?   For the complete
cleansing of our hearts of all hatred, and variance,
and emulation, and wrath, and strife, and envy,
and such like ?   Is there, this morning of God,
within the walls of this House of God, one man
who last night knocked and knocked, and returned
after he was in bed and half asleep, and knocked
again for more love, for more long-suffering, for
more gentleness, for more meekness ?   For a clean
heart ?   For a heart clean of envy and ill-will ?
For a heart dead to sin, and to his own besetting
and indwelling sin ?   Is there one ?   My brethren,
God is your witness : for the darkness hideth not
from Him : but the night shineth before Him as
the day.   " But, thou, when thou prayest, enter
into thy closet, and when thou hast shut thy door,
pray to thy Father, Which seeth in secret ; and thy
Father Which seeth in secret shall reward thee
openly."   When the Books are opened—that is to
say.   When your secret place of prayer is opened.
When your midnight is no longer.   When the Holy
Spirit has finished His midnight work in you.   As
you pray at midnight, in the thick, and dark, and
lonely, and slothful, and all-men-asleep midnight
of this evil life, so shall it be answered and fulfilled
to you in the morning.   Only, understand, and be

instructed—not till the morning.   Understand this
well, that you will get earnests and foretastes before
the morning,—but they will only be earnests and
foretastes.   Submit to this and lay it to heart,
that the full answer to your best prayer is not given
in this life.   You will get the full answer to all your
other prayers in this life.   Peace with Esau : long
life, and riches, and the lives of your enemies :
corn, and wine, and oil : what you shall eat, and
what you shall drink, and wherewithal you shall
be clothed.   But if your heart is carried on to pray
for the Holy Spirit, and for the Holy Spirit alone,
you will have to continue in prayer till the morning.
Every man in his own order, and in his own time.
But then,—when the day breaks :

"What are these which are arrayed in white
robes, and whence came they ? . . . They shall
hunger no more, neither thirst any more. . . . For
the Lamb which is in the midst of the Throne shall
feed them, and shall lead them unto living fountains
of waters : and God shall wipe away all tears from
their eyes."   Amen.

PART III

SOME ASPECTS OF THE WAY OF PRAYER

XV

PRAYER TO THE MOST HIGH

" Lord, teach us to pray."—LUKE xi. 1.
" They return, but not to the Most High."—Hos. vii. 16.

THE Most High. The High and Lofty One, That
inhabiteth eternity, whose Name is Holy. The
King Eternal, Immortal, Invisible, the Only Wise
God. The Blessed and Only Potentate, the King
of kings, and Lord of lords: Who only hath immortality, dwelling in the light which no man can
approach unto: Whom no man hath seen, nor can
see. Great and marvellous are Thy works, Lord
God Almighty : just and true are Thy ways, Thou
King of saints. Who shall not fear Thee, O Lord,
and glorify Thy Name? For Thou only art Holy.
God is a Spirit: Infinite, Eternal, and Unchange-
able in His Being, Wisdom, Power, Holiness, Justice,
Goodness and Truth. Lo! these are parts of His
ways : but how little a portion is heard of Him !
But the thunder of His power who can understand?
The Most High !

Now the greatness of God is the true index and
measure of the greatness of man. God made man
in His own image. God made man for Himself,

and not for any end short of Himself. " Man's
chief end is to glorify God, and to enjoy Him for
ever." " In Thy presence is fulness of joy : at
Thy right hand there are pleasures for evermore."
" Then will I go unto the altar of God, unto God
my exceeding joy." " Enter thou into the joy of
thy Lord." The higher, then, that God is, the
higher is our everlasting destination to be. The
more blessed God is, the more blessed are we pur-
posed and predestinated to be. The more sur-
passing all imagination of Prophets and Psalmists
and Apostles the Divine Nature is,—the more true
it is that eye hath not seen, nor ear heard, nor hath
it entered into the heart of man what God hath
prepared for them who are for ever to be made
partakers of the Divine Nature. " I in them, and
Thou in Me. And the glory which Thou gavest
Me, I have given them : that the Love wherewith
Thou hast loved Me may be in them : and I in
them." And then, in order to hedge up, and secure,
all these to their everlasting exaltation and blessedness, God has made it the supreme law of all His
laws to us, that all men shall, above all things
else, seek their own chief end. And He has made
it the sin of sins, the one unpardonable sin, in any
man, to come short of his chief end—which is the
full enjoying of God to all eternity. And the
prophet Hosea has all that in his mind, and in his
heart, when he utters that great evangelical invita-

tion and encouragement, " Come and let us return
unto the Lord." And he has all that in his mind
and in his heart also, when he utters the sore
lamentation and bitter accusation of the text,
" They return, but not to the Most High."

Now it is necessary to know, and ever to keep
in mind, that prayer is the all-comprehending name
that is given to every step in our return to God.
True prayer, the richest and the ripest prayer, the
most acceptable and the most prevailing prayer,
embraces many elements : it is made up of many
operations of the mind, and many motions of the
heart. To begin to come to ourselves,—however
far off we may then discover ourselves to be,—to
begin to think about ourselves, is already to begin
to pray. To begin to feel fear, or shame, or remorse, or a desire after better things, is to begin
to pray. To say within ourselves, " I will arise
and go to my Father,"—that is to begin to pray.
To see what we are, and to desire to turn from
what we are—that also is to pray. In short, every
such thought about ourselves, and about God, and
about sin and its wages, and about salvation, its
price and its preciousness ; every foreboding
thought about death and judgment and heaven
and hell ; every reflection about the blood and
righteousness of Jesus Christ ; and every wish of
our hearts that we were more like Jesus Christ :
all our reading of the Word. all our meditation,

reflection, contemplation, prostration and adoration ; all faith, all hope, all love ; all that, and all of that same kind,—it all comes, with the most perfect truth and propriety, under the all-embracing name of " prayer " ; it all enters into the all-absorbing life of prayer.

> Prayer is the soul's sincere desire,
>   Uttered or unexpressed :
> The motion of a hidden fire
>   That trembles in the breast.
>
> Prayer is the burden of a sigh,
>   The falling of a tear,
> The upward glancing of an eye
>   When none but God is near.
>
> Prayer is the simplest form of speech
>   That infant lips can try :
> Prayer the sublimest strains that reach
>   The Majesty on High.

How noble then is prayer ! How incomparably noble ! Who would not be a man of prayer ? What wise, what sane man, will continue to neglect prayer ? " Ask, and it shall be given you ; that your joy may be full."

Now, be it understood that neither this text, nor this sermon, is addressed to those who do not pray. Both the prophet and the preacher have their eye this morning on those who not only pray, on occasion, but who also are at pains to perform all those other exercises of mind and heart that enter into prayer. They read the Word of God : they meditate on what they read : they sing God's praise, at

home and in the sanctuary; and they repent and
reform their life. What more would this prophet
have than that? My brethren, this is what he
would have: he would have all that done *to God*.
The prophets are all full of this very same accusation, and remonstrance, and protest, that all the
acts prescribed by the law of God were done: but,
not being done to God, the most scrupulous, the
most punctual, the most expensive service was no
service at all in God's sight and estimation. " To
what purpose is the multitude of your sacrifices
unto Me? saith the Lord. When ye come to
appear before Me, who hath required this at your
hands, to tread My courts? Bring no more vain
oblations: incense is an abomination unto Me:
the new moons and Sabbaths I cannot away with:
it is iniquity, even the solemn meeting. Your new
moons and your appointed feasts My soul hateth.
They are a trouble unto Me: I am weary to bear
them." That is the climax, indeed, of all such
accusations and indignations; but all the prophets
are full of the same accusation; and it is all summed
up in the short and sharp accusation of the text,
" They return, but not to the Most High."

But then on the other hand, we are very happy
in having the other side of this matter most im-
pressively and most instructively set before us in a
multitude of most precious psalms. And it is this
indeed that makes the Psalms the mother and the

model of all subsequent books of true devotion:
because we see in them those true and spiritual
worshippers in Israel returning, and returning to
the Most High.   Take one of those truly returning
Psalmists, and hear him, and imitate him. " Against
Thee, Thee only, have I sinned, and done this evil
in Thy sight.   Wash me throughly from mine
iniquity, and cleanse me from my sin.   Behold,
Thou desirest truth in the inward parts : and in
the hidden part Thou shalt make me to know
wisdom.   Hide Thy face from my sins : and blot
out all mine iniquities.   Create in me a clean heart,
O God : and renew a right spirit within me.   Cast
me not away from Thy presence : and take not Thy
Holy Spirit from me.   The sacrifices of God are a
broken spirit : a broken and a contrite heart, O
God, Thou wilt not despise."   That, my brethren,
is true returning to God.   And God meets all such
returnings, and says, " Come now and let us reason
together : though your sins be as scarlet, they shall
be as white as snow : though they be red like
crimson, they shall be as wool."

Now, while we have all that in the Old Testament,
for our direction, and for our imitation, and for our
encouragement, we, New Testament men, are met
at every step of our return to God with this great
utterance of our Lord on this whole matter : " No
man cometh unto the Father but by Me."   And,
no sooner have we heard that,—no sooner do we

believe that,—than every step of our return to the
Most High from that day takes on a new direction.
All our religious exercises, public and private, are
now directed towards Him of whom the Apostle
says, " He dwelt among us, and we have heard, we
have seen with our eyes, we have looked upon, and
our hands have handled, of the word of life.   That
which we have seen and heard declare we unto you,
that ye also may have fellowship with us."   Fellowship, that is, in their fellowship with the Word
made flesh, till he that hath seen and heard the Son,
has as good as seen and heard the Father ; and
till all our prayers and praises are to be directed, in
the first place, to the Word made flesh, even as in the
Old Testament they were directed immediately and
only to the Most High.   But, with all our New Testament nearness to God ; with the Most High, now and
for ever, in our own nature ; with Jesus Christ, the
one Mediator between God and man, near to every
one of us,—are we any better of all that ?   When
we return in prayer and in praise, do we return into
the very presence of Jesus Christ ?   Or are we,
with all that, as far from Him as the formalists in
Israel were far from the Most High ?   Have we
taken any real assistance, and any true advantage,
out of the Incarnation in this matter of prayer ?
The Incarnation of the Son of God has brought
many assistances and many advantages to the
children of men : and one of the greatest and most

momentous is this,—that the Most High is now so
near us : and especially so near us when we pray.
Now, is that so ? As a matter of experience and
practice is that so to us ? Do we practise the
presence of Christ when we pray ? Do we think
ourselves and imagine ourselves into His presence
when we stand up to sing, and kneel down to pray ?
Have we as keen, and as quick, and as intense, and
as ever-present a sense of His presence as we have
of the presence of our fellow-worshippers ? When,
at any time, we kneel in secret, is it no longer secret
as it once was ; but is the whole place now peopled
with the presence of Christ ? And, in public worship,
are we so overshadowed and overawed with His
presence that all those fellow-worshippers around
us are, for the time, but so many mere shadows to
us ? Is it so ? Is it becoming so ? It will assuredly
be so when we return to Jesus Christ in our prayers,
and when He presents us and our returning prayers
to the Most High.

Speaking for myself,—I have found this device
very helpful in my own returnings to my Saviour.
And I recommend this same device to you. Make
great use of the Four Gospels in your efforts to
return to Jesus Christ. Think that you are living
in Jerusalem. Think that you are one of the
Twelve. Think that you are one of those amazing
people who had Him in their streets, and in their
homes, every day. And fall down before Him as

they did. Speak to Him as they did. Show Him
your palsies and your leprosies as they did. Follow
Him about, telling Him about your sons and
daughters as they did. Tell Him that you have a
child nigh unto death as they did. Wash His feet
with your tears, and wipe them with the hair of
your head, as they did. Work your way through
the Four Gospels, from end to end : and, all the
time, with a great exercise of faith, believe that He
is as much with you as He was with Simon the leper,
and with the Syro-Phœnician woman, and with Mary
Magdalene, and with Lazarus who had been four
days dead, and with the thief on the cross. Read,
and believe, and pray. Fall at His feet. Look
up in His face. Put Him in remembrance. Put
your finger on the very place, and ask Him if that is
really true. Ask Him if He did and said that.
Ask Him if you are really to believe that, and are
safe, in your case also, to act upon that. If you
are a scholar, say to yourself as the old scholarly
believers said,—*Deus ubique est et totus ubique est*;
and set out again to return to God in Christ in the
strength of that. And, if you are an unlearned
and an ignorant man, like Peter and John, well,
like them say,—" Were not these His words to us
while He was yet with us,—Lo, I am with you
alway, even to the end of the world." And act
your faith again, as if it was indeed so. And the
more pure, and naked, and absolute faith you put

in Him, and into your prayer,—the more will He take pleasure in you, till He will say to you : " O woman ! Woman ! I have not found so great faith, no, not in all Israel. Be it unto thee and unto thy daughter, even as thou wilt ! " " I came to this at last," says a great Scottish saint,—" I came at last to this, that I would not rise and go away till I felt sure I had had an audience. And I sometimes felt as sure that I was having an audience as if He had been before me in the body."

But, before he came to that, he often said,—and the saying has become classical in the North of Scotland,—lamenting his parched heart he often said, " Surely I have laid my pipe far short of the fountain." And so he had. And so have we. No words could describe our case better than the text, and that other saying so like the text, For we also are always returning ; but not to the Most High. We are always laying our pipe, but not up to the fountain. We are always engaged in the exercises of public and private religion. We are not atheists. We are not scoffers. We do not forsake the assembling of ourselves together. We are glad when it is said to us,—Let us go up to the House of the Lord. We enter into His courts with thanksgiving, and into His gates with praise. At the time appointed, we partake of the Lord's Supper ; and, again, we bring our children to be baptized. We make our vow, and we pay it.

And when at any time we fall into a besetting sin, we hasten to repent and to reform our lives. We incline our hearts again to keep God's commandments.

But, with all that, this so heart-searching, this so soul-exacting text discovers us, and condemns us. We return to all that; but we do not return to the Most High. We lay our pipe up to divine ordinances, —to the most spiritual of divine ordinances : up to prayer, and to praise, and to meditation, and to Sabbaths and to sacraments : but, all the time, all these things are but so many cisterns. All these things, taken together, are not the Fountain. God is the Fountain. And when we return to God, when we lay our pipe up to the true Fountain of living waters,—then we taste an immediateness of communion, and an inwardness of consolation, and a strength of assurance, and a solidity of peace, and a fulness of joy, that are known to those only who truly return to the Most High. Until we are able to say,—and that not out of a great psalm only but much more out of a great personal and indisputable experience,—" Whom have I in heaven but Thee ? and there is none upon earth that I desire beside Thee. My flesh and my heart faileth : but God is the strength of my heart, and my portion for ever."

XVI

THE COSTLINESS OF PRAYER

"Lord, teach us to pray."—LUKE xi. 1.
"And ye shall seek Me, and find Me, when ye shall search for Me with all your heart."—JER. xxix. 13.

IN his fine book on Benefits, Seneca says that nothing is so costly to us as that is which we purchase by prayer. When we come on that hard-to-be-understood saying of his for the first time, we set it down as another of the well-known paradoxes of the Stoics. For He who is far more to us than all the Stoics taken together has said to us on the subject of prayer,—"Ask, and it shall be given you; seek, and ye shall find; knock, and it shall be opened unto you." Now what could possibly be cheaper than just asking? And what could cost us less than just to knock at God's door? And yet, when we see such stern and self-denying souls as Dante and Teresa setting their seals to Seneca's startling words, that makes us stop and think whether there may not be much more in the Stoic's paradoxical words about the cost of prayer than lies on the surface. And when we do stop and think on the whole subject of prayer, and especially on the costliness of prayer, such things as these begin to be impressed upon us.

1. To begin with: Our habits of prayer come to cost us no little *time*. We usually divide our day of twenty-four hours in this way,—eight hours for work; eight hours for meals, and rest, and recreation; and eight hours for sleep. You will observe that it is not said where reading, and meditation, and prayer come in. And the reason of that is because, with most men, these things do not come in at all. But, in revenge, when reading and meditation and prayer do once begin to come in on a man, they make great inroads both upon his hours of work, and his hours of recreation, and even upon his hours of sleep. It is not that the Hearer of prayer has any need of our hours: He has no pleasure in taxing our time, either during the day, or during the night. The truth is,—time does not enter into His side of this matter at all. He has always plenty of time. He inhabits eternity. He is always waiting to be gracious. It is we who need time to prepare our hearts to seek God. And it takes some men a long, and a retired, and an uninterrupted time to get their minds and their hearts into the true frame for prayer and for the presence of God. And it is this that makes the night-time so suitable to some men for sacred reading, for devout meditation, and for secret prayer. Our time is now our own. Our day's

work is now done. Our door is now shut. And no one will intrude upon us, or will in any way interfere with us, at this time of night. Till from such experiences as these, as life goes on, we come to discover that time, pure time, is as indispensable and as important an element in all true prayer as is repentance, or faith, or reformation itself. Indeed, without a liberal allowance of time, no man has ever attained to a real life of prayer at all. So much is that the case, that Seneca might quite safely have descended into particulars, and might very well have said that prayer costs so much time that, instead of a few stolen moments now and then, it takes from some men all that remains of their time on this earth. Now that cannot, surely, be said to be bought cheaply, which despoils us of so much of the most precious thing we possess ; and a thing, moreover, which is so fast running short with so many of us.

2. Time and *Thought*. I do not say that a man must bring immense and commanding powers of thought to prayer before he can succeed in it. But I do say that those who do possess immense and commanding powers of thought must bring all their powers of thought to bear upon their prayers, if they would be accepted and answered. Almighty God is infinitely the greatest and grandest subject of thought and imagination in all the Universe : and yet there is nothing in all the Universe to which

most men give less thought and less imagination
than to Almighty God. Joseph Butler told Dr.
Samuel Clarke that the Being and the Nature of
God had been his incessant study ever since he
began to think at all. And, further on in life, he
said that, to his mind, Divinity was, of all our
studies, the most suitable for a reasonable nature.
Now, not philosophers, and theologians, and
moralists like Bishop Butler only, but all God's
people, must cultivate Butler's habits of thought,
if they have any ambition to please God greatly,
and to make real progress in the life of prayer
Take any man of prayer you like, and you will see
Butler's noble habit of mind exhibited and illustrated in that man. Take the Psalmists,—what
wealth of devotional thought there is in the Psalms !
Take the 17th of John,—what heights and depths of
heavenly thought there are in that single chapter !
Take Paul's intercessory prayers for the Ephesians
and the Colossians,—and what majesty and
Christological thought is there also ! Take
Augustine and Andrewes, and see how they will
exercise not your powers of thought only but all
that is within you. To come back to Paul—that
man of time and thought in prayer, if ever there
was one : " Now unto the King Eternal, Immortal,
Invisible, the Only Wise God." And again : " The
Blessed and Only Potentate, the King of kings,
and Lord of lords. Who only hath immortality,

dwelling in the light which no man can approach
unto : Whom no man hath seen, nor can see."
What mortal man has powers of thought at all
equal to such doxologies as these ? No man, no
angel : no, not the Incarnate Son Himself. And
what schoolmaster, in Sabbath school, or day
school, can himself grasp all this answer to his own
question—" God is a Spirit, Infinite, Eternal, and
Unchangeable, in His Being, Wisdom, Power,
Holiness, Justice, Goodness and Truth " ?   Try
your own compass and grasp of thought on such
matters as these ; and say if Seneca was not wholly
in the right when he said that nothing is so severe
upon a man's powers of thought and imagination
and heart as just to approach God, and to abide for
a sufficient time before God, in prayer.   No wonder
that we often fall asleep through sheer exhaustion
of body and mind, when we begin to give something
like adequate time and thought to meditation,
adoration, prayer and praise.

3. But both time and thought are easy, pleasant
and costless compared with this,—*Thy will be done.*
To say " Thy will be done," when we enter our
Gethsemane,—that throws us on our faces on the
earth : that brings the blood to our brows.   And
yet at no less cost than that was God's own Son
" heard in that He feared."   When some one, far
dearer to us than our own souls, is laid down on
his death-bed, to say " Not my will, but Thine be

done,"—at what a cost is that said in such an hour !
What a heart-racking price has to be paid for that
prayer ! And yet, pay that price we must : pour
out our hearts into that prayer we must, if we are,
like our Lord, to be made perfect by suffering.
And not at death-beds only, but at times that are
worse than death,—times upon which I will not
trust myself to put words. Times also, when a
great cloud of disappointment and darkness gathers
over our life : when some great hope is for ever
blasted : when some great opportunity and expectation is for ever gone, and never to return.
To lie down before God's feet and say, " Not my
will, but Thine be done," at such times—at what
a cost is that said and done ! And to say it without bitterness, or gloom, or envy, or ill-will at any
one : and to go on to the end of our lonely and
desolate life, full of love and service to God and
man,—at such a sight as that, God says, " This
is My Beloved Son, in Whom I am well pleased !
Come up hither. Inherit the kingdom prepared for
thee before the foundation of the world ! "

4. And, then, as to how we have to pay down all
our transgressions and secret sins before our
prayers will be heard,—let one speak who has
gone deeper into that matter than any one else I
know. " Now," she says, " I saw that there would
be no answer to me till I had entire purity of
conscience, and no longer regarded any iniquity

whatsoever in my heart. I saw that there were
some secret affections still left in me that were
spoiling all. I passed nearly twenty years of my
life on this stormy sea, constantly tossed with the
tempests of my own heart, and never nearing the
harbour. I had no sweetness in God, and certainly
no sweetness in sin. All my tears did not hold me
back from sin when the opportunity returned; till
I came to look on my tears as little short of a delusion. And yet they were not a delusion. It was
the goodness of the Lord to give me such com-
punction, even when it was not, as yet, accom-
panied with complete reformation. But the whole
root of my evil lay in my not thoroughly avoiding
all occasions and opportunities of sin. I spent
eighteen years in that miserable attempt to reconcile God and my life of sin. Now, out of all
that, I will say to you,"—she continues,—" never
cease from prayer, be your life ever so bad. Prayer
is the only way to amend your life : and, without
prayer, it will never be mended. I ought to have
utterly and thoroughly distrusted, and suspected,
and detested myself. I sought for help. I sometimes took great pains to get help. But I did not
understand of how little use all that is unless we
utterly root out all confidence in ourselves, and
place our confidence at once, and for ever, and
absolutely, in God. Those were eighteen most
miserable years with me." But we do not need to

go beyond our own Bibles for all that. For we have in our own Bibles these well-known words of David : " If I regard iniquity in my heart, the Lord will not hear me. But, verily, God hath heard me : He hath attended to the voice of my prayer. Blessed be God which hath not turned away my prayer, nor His mercy from me."

5. And, not to go the length of gross sins, either secret, or open, or long-continued, prayer when you once take it in dead earnest, and as for your immortal soul,—such prayer will cost you all your soft, and easy, and slothful, and self-indulgent habits. I will not go on to name any of your soft, and easy, and slothful, and self-indulgent habits. But you know them yourselves and your conscience will not be slow in naming them to you, if you will let her speak out. Seneca is always telling young Lucilius to make up his mind. To make up his mind whether he is to be one of God's athletes or no. To make up his mind as the athletes of the arena do. They make up their mind to deny themselves in eating and drinking : in lounging all day in the Campus Martius and in soaking themselves all night in taverns: and on the day of the arena they have their reward. You have the same thing in the Epistle to the Hebrews : " Wherefore, seeing we also are compassed about with so great a cloud of witnesses, let us lay aside every weight, and the sin which doth so easily beset us, and let

us run with patience the race that is set before us."
And again in Corinthians : " Know ye not that
they which run in a race run all, but one receiveth
the prize? And every man that striveth for the
mastery is temperate in all things. Now they do
it to obtain a corruptible crown : but we an in-
corruptible. But I keep under my body, and
bring it into subjection : lest that by any means,
when I have preached to others, I myself should be
a castaway." " Do I pray," demands Andrewes
of himself, " do I pray—if not seven times a day,
as David, yet at least three times a day as Daniel ?
If not, as Solomon, at length, yet shortly, as the
publican ? If not like Christ, the whole night, at
least for one hour ? If not on the ground and in
ashes, at least not in my bed ? If not in sackcloth,
at least not in purple and fine linen ? If not altogether freed from all other desires, at least freed
from all immoderate, unclean and unholy desires ? "
O true and self-denying saints of God,—shall we
ever be found worthy to touch so much as your
shoe-latchet ?

In short, on this whole subject, and to sum up on
it,—prayer, in all its exacting costliness, is like
nothing so much as it is like faith and love. It is
like Paul's faith, which made him suffer the loss of
all things, and made him count all his best things
but as so much dung, that he might win Christ, and
be found in Him. Prayer is like love also,—that

most vehement and most all-consuming of all the passions of the human heart. Prayer is like the love of the bride in the song : " Set me as a seal upon thine heart, as a seal upon thine arm : for love is strong as death : jealousy is cruel as the grave : the coals thereof are coals of fire, which hath a most vehement flame. Many waters cannot quench love, neither can the floods drown it : if a man would give all the substance of his house for love, it would utterly be contemned." And so it is with prayer. And even with all that, the half of the price of prayer has not been told. For, after we have paid down all that immense price for prayer, and for the things that come to us by prayer, the things we paid so much for are not to be called our own after all. We have still to hold them, and enjoy them, in a life of prayer and praise. Even as we got those good things by prayer at first, so we have to hold them by prayer to the end. It is as Samuel Rutherford has it in his rare classic entitled *Christ Dying*. " It is better," says that eminent saint, " to hold your lands by prayer than by your own industry, or by conquest, or by inheritance, or by right of redemption. Have you wife, child, houses, lands, wisdom, honour, learning, parts, grace, godliness ? See to it how you got them. For, if you got them not by prayer at the first, you do not hold them either righteously, or safely, or with the true enjoyment of them. See that you

get a new charter to them all by continual and
believing prayer. Hold and enjoy all your pos-
sessions by continual and believing prayer and
praise."

Stand forth, then, all you who are men of much
prayer. Stand forth, and say whether or no the
wise Stoic was right when he said that nothing
is so costly, so exorbitant, so extortionate, as that
is which is bought by prayer. While, on the other
hand, nothing is so truly and everlastingly enriching
as that is which is gotten and held by prayer, and
by prayer alone.

Lord, teach us to pray. Lord ! Lord !

XVII

REVERENCE IN PRAYER

" Lord, teach us to pray."—LUKE xi. 1.
" Offer it now unto thy governor ; will he be pleased with thee
or accept thy person ? saith the Lord of Hosts."—MAL. i. 8.

IF we were summoned to dine, or to any other
audience, with our sovereign, with what fear and
trembling should we prepare ourselves for the
ordeal ! Our fear at the prospect before us would
take away all our pride, and all our pleasure, in the
great honour that had come to us.   And how careful
we should be to prepare ourselves, in every possible
way, for the great day ! We should at once bethink
ourselves of those men of our acquaintance who had
been at court, and we should throw ourselves on
them to tell us everything.   How to answer the
royal command : how to dress : how to drive up to
the gate : who would meet us : how they would
know us : all about the entrances, and the stairs,
and the rooms : all about Her Majesty herself and
the royal table.   And then, when the day and the
hour came,—our first sight of the Queen,[1] and her
first sight of us ! And then, our name announced,

[1] This sermon was preached in 1899.

till our heart beat as never before. And then our seat at the table : and what to say, and what not to say. And, at the end of the day, our thankfulness that we had been carried through the ordeal so well, and without any dreadful mistake.

Now, all that is, as near as can be, the meaning of Malachi in the text. The prophet is protesting against the scandalous irreverence, and the open profanity, of the people of Israel in their approaches to Almighty God. " Offer it now to thy governor ! " he cries to them. " Will he be pleased with such service at thy hands ? Or will he accept thee ? A son honoureth his father, and a servant his master If then I be a father, where is Mine honour ? And if I be a master, where is My fear ? saith the Lord of Hosts. I have no pleasure in you, saith the Lord of Hosts, neither will I accept an offering at your hand."

1. Now, to begin with, let us take this pungent passage, and apply it to our own public worship, to the place where we are now assembled, and to the service we are now engaged in. Compare the stateliness, the orderliness, the rich beauty, the impressive silence, the nobleness, the reverential love of the Queen's palace : compare all that with the squalor, the disorder, the absence of all beauty, the rude noises, the universal irreverence, I will not say of this church, but of so many churches up and down the land. And if, in some outward

things, there has been some improvement for some time past among us, how do we ourselves stand individually, for inward improvement, for our personal demeanour of mind and heart in public worship ? A Court chaplain, who is at the same time a minister of a congregation, says this to his congregation, " When you are in an audience with your sovereign, would you have your mind taken up all the time with impertinent and utterly trifling things ? When you are standing, or kneeling, in the royal presence, would you turn to see who is coming in when the door opens ? Would you rise and look out to see who is passing the window ? Would you stare round the room at the servants, and at the furniture, while your sovereign is speaking to you, and you to him ? " And so on. No. The thing is inconceivable. No sane man could possibly do such a thing. There is a good story told at the expense of a certain enterprising and unceremonious English journalist, to the effect that the Czar returned to his councillors, and said that he had just passed through an experience that was new to him,—he had been " dismissed " by a newspaper man as soon as the interview was over. Both Malachi, and the Court chaplain, and the story about the dismissal of the Czar, have lessons for us all about our behaviour in public worship.

And, the worst of it is that all this irreverence,

disrespect for the House of God, and, indeed, down-
right profanity, begins where it should be arrested
and denounced till it becomes impossible. For it
begins and is perpetuated, of all places, in the pulpit.
With how little reverence and godly fear do we
who are ministers enter the pulpit! With plenty
of fear, if not reverence, of man. Full of the fear
of man, lest we do not come up to-day to what our
irreverent people expect of us. How we study
and prepare to pray, and to preach, setting mortal
men like you before us! Were it not that He,
with Whom we have to do, is, far past all His
promises, "long-suffering and slow to wrath"
towards us ministers, an angry Voice would many
a Sabbath morning cut short our profane per-
formances with the sentence,—"O graceless
minister! Offer all that to thy governor!" And,
thus it comes about,—"Like priest, like people."
For who, here, of all this multitude of people with
psalm-books in their hands, really sang this morning's psalm to God? To God? Who set everything else aside at the church door, because he was
to have one more audience of the King, Eternal,
Immortal, Invisible? Who prayed to God, in the
opening or in the intercessory prayer, with an
arrested, entranced and enraptured heart? No:
not one. "Take it to your governor."

2. And, beginning with public worship, we take
all that profanity home with us to our family

worship. For one thing,—all our family worship is made to give place, morning and night, to anything and everything. There are so-called Christian homes where the sons and the daughters and the guests come down to family worship just as they please and find it convenient. If they are down in time for breakfast, good and well—the kitchen arrangements must not be disturbed; but the family prayers to God may be observed or not as our young gentlemen please. And, as to evening prayers,—this actually happened in one of our own houses the other night. A new servant-man brought in the books, and laid them on the table in the crowded drawing-room, at the usual hour. I should have said it was the night of a large and late dinner-party. The poor innocent fellow narrowly escaped being sent about his business as soon as the last guest had left. "Do you not know, sir"—his master set upon him—"that in good society there is never family prayers after a party like what we have had to-night?" The stupid man had just come from a devout old castle in the Highlands, and did not know that family worship was a fast-dying-out ceremony in the West End society he had come to serve.

But even when family worship is never,—morning nor night—pushed into a corner, it might almost better be. The regulation chapter; the wooden monotony; the mechanical round; the absence

of a thought, or an idea, or an emotion, or a feeling ;
one pushing about a creaking chair when he is on
his knees : another yawning till the whole room
is ashamed of the indecency : another coughing
and sneezing without ceremony : and then,—before
Amen is well uttered,—all the room beginning to talk
at once : it had been so bottled up for the past
ten minutes. I only know one house, in all my
acquaintance, where ordinary decorum is taught
to the children and the guests in the matter of a
moment of reverential silence before the Babel
begins again after prayer to God. Now, would you
cough in the Queen's face ? Would you yawn till
she heard you ? Would you up, and begin to talk
to her servants before they are well off their knees ?
" Take it now unto thy governor."

Very few men are such well-mannered gentlemen
at home as they are in company. No man dresses
for his wife and children, as all men so scrupulously
dress for court and ceremonial. But some select
men do. They have a queen every evening at
home, and young princes and princesses at table
with them. And they have their reward. And so
in the matter of family prayers. Few men, ministers
or others, prepare themselves for family prayers as
they do for State services, and ceremonial devotions. But some men do : and they, too, have
their reward. Thomas Boston made it a rule to
prepare himself for family worship, as regularly,

and as honestly, as for the pulpit or the prayer-
meeting. And he had his remarkable rewards, as
you will see when you read his remarkable *Memoirs*
of himself. An old college friend of mine keeps
me posted up with the work of grace that always
goes on in his congregation, and in his family.
And, not long ago, I had a letter from him telling
me that God had given him the soul of another of
his children : and the best of it was that it took
place at, and sprang out of, the family worship of
the manse. You and I would be taken aback if
any one—a child, a servant, a guest—said to us
that they had ever been any the better of any
family worship of ours. We do not expect it. We
do not prepare for it. We do not really wish it.
And we do not get it. And we never shall.

But it is perhaps at the breakfast and the dinner
table that our family mockery of God comes to its
most perfect performance. This is the way they
said grace about the year 1720 in England. " In
one house you may perhaps see the head of the
house just pulling off his hat : in another, half
getting up from his seat : another shall, it may be,
proceed as far as to make as if he said something,
but was ashamed of what he said," and so on. You
will see the miserable picture finished when you go
home to-day. And you will see the heartless
mockery to perfection the first public dinner you
are at. I suppose this is what Malachi meant

when he said, " Even the Lord's meat is to you contemptible."

3. And then, secret prayer, " closet " prayer, as Christ calls it,—even where there is a certain semblance of it,—take it to thy governor ! For are not these its characters and features, even where it in some measure exists ? Its chanciness, its fitfulness, its occasionliness, its shortness, even curtness, its hastiness to get it over, and to get away from it, and from Him ; and so on. " Be not so hasty," says the prophet, " to get out of His sight "; showing, you see, that in secret prayer they had the very same impiety and profanity to contend with that we have. And, again : " If the spirit of thy ruler rise up against thee, leave not thy place." No : leave not thy place, for His spirit rises up against all haste to get rid of Him and all dislike at His presence, and all distaste, and all restraint of prayer. " Leave not thy place." The whole world is in that word. Thy soul is in that word. Thy salvation, and the salvation of others, is in that word to thee, " Leave not thy place." No ! Leave not thy place. Keep firm on thy knees. Go back a second and a third time. Even after thou art out of thy door, if the Spirit moves thee : and more, if He has forsaken thee and does not move thee, go back : shut thy door upon thee again : for thy Governor is there waiting for thee, and nothing in thee pleases Him like secret prayer.

And, sometimes, speak out when you are alone with
Him. You will find it a great assistance to a
languid faith sometimes to speak out. Cry aloud
to Him sometimes. You will find a mighty alteration in your heart as you continue, and continue, in
secret, and in intimate and in confiding prayer.
Say to yourself that the Governor of heaven and
earth is shut in with you, and you with Him ; and
be not in such a hurry to " dismiss " Him.

Now, this Royal command has again gone forth
among us concerning next Lord's Day. " If the
Lord will, the Sacrament of the Lord's Supper will
be dispensed here." " The Mighty God, even the
Lord, hath spoken. Out of Zion, the perfection
of beauty, God hath shined. Gather my saints
together unto ME; those that have made a
covenant with Me by sacrifice." And in obedience
to His command we shall all be gathering together
to the Lord's Table about this hour next Lord's
Day. Now, let us just do—all this week—as if
it were the week before we were to go to Windsor
or to Balmoral. Let us think all the week about
our King, and about His Table, and about how
we should prepare ourselves for His Table; and
how we should behave ourselves at it. Let us seek
out those royal favourites who are at home at the
Lord's Table, and go by their advice. There are
books, also, of court etiquette, that are simply
invaluable to intending communicants,—golden

books, in which the ways of heaven are set forth, and illustrated, for the counsel and guidance of new beginners. Read nothing else all the week. Fill your mind with the ways and words and manners of the Royal Table. And be ready, with the right words to speak, when the King speaks to you. And when He comes in to see the guests, He will see you with your wedding garment on : and He will look on you with His Royal countenance, and will say to you, " Eat, O friends ! drink, yea, drink abundantly, O beloved." And you will call the name of this place Peniel : for you will say, " I have seen God face to face, and my life is preserved."

XVIII

THE PLEADING NOTE IN PRAYER

" Lord, teach us to pray."—LUKE xi. 1.
" Let us plead together."—ISA. xliii. 26.

WE all know quite well what it is to " plead together." We all plead with one another every day. We all understand the exclamation of the patriarch Job quite well—" O that one might plead for a man with God, as a man pleadeth for his neighbour." We have a special order of men among ourselves who do nothing else but plead with the judge for their neighbours. We call those men by the New Testament name of advocates : and a much-honoured and a much-sought-after office is the office of an advocate. But, what if in this also, " earth be but the shadow of heaven : and things therein each to other like, more than on earth is thought " ?

Prayer, in its most comprehensive sense, embraces many states of the mind, and many movements and manifestations of the heart. But our use of the word prayer this morning will be limited to these two elements in all true prayer—petition and pleading.

Petitioning and pleading are two quite distinct things. When we make a petition, we simply ask that something shall be granted and given to us. Whereas when we plead, we show reasons why our petition should be granted and given. Petitioning is asking : whereas pleading is arguing. When a petitioner is in dead earnest, he is not content with merely tabling his petition. He does not simply state his bare case, and then leave it to speak for itself. No. Far from that. He at once proceeds to support his case with all the reasons and arguments and appeals that he can command. His naked petition, he knows quite well, is not enough. And thus it is that, like Job, he hastens to " order his cause before God, and to fill his mouth with arguments."

Now, as was to be expected, we find that Holy Scripture is full not only of petitioning but of pleading also. Especially the Psalms. Then, again, Job is an extraordinary book in many respects ; but in nothing is it more extraordinary than just in its magnificent speeches of argumentation and pleading, both with God and with man. So much so, that a young advocate could study no finer model of the loftiest rhetoric of his great profession than just the passionate pleadings and appeals of which this splendid book is so full. And then, most wonderful of all, most instructive, most impressive, and most heart-consoling of all, the

17th of John is full of this same element of reasoning and pleading,—more full of reasoning and
pleading, remarkable to discover, than even of
petitioning.   Three petitions, or at most four, are
all that our Lord makes to His Father in that great
audience of His.   And then, all the rest of His time
and strength, in that great audience, is taken up
with pleadings and arguments and reasonings and
appeals,—as to why His four petitions for Himself,
and for His disciples, should be heard and answered.

And then, the pleas, so to call them, that are
employed by the prophets and the psalmists,—and
much more by our Lord Himself,—are not only
so many argumentative pleas ; they are absolutely
a whole, and an extraordinarily rich, theology in
themselves.   The warrants they all build upon ;
the justifications they all put forward ; the reasons
they all assign why they should be heard and
answered,—all these things are a fine study in the
very deepest divinity.   The things in God and in
themselves that all those petitioners put forward ;
the allegations and pretexts they advance ; the
refuges they run into ; and the grounds they take
their last stand upon,—the prayers of God's great
saints are not only a mine for a divinity student
to work down to the bottom, but they are an incomparable education to every practitioner of the
advocate's art.   And if they are indisputably all
that, then much more are those inspired prayers the

very best meditation and ensample to every throne-besieging sinner, and to every importuning saint. For those great suppliants plead before God, God Himself : they plead the Divine Nature and the Divine Name : they plead, and put God in remembrance of what He can do, and what He cannot do : they plead themselves, and their depraved and debilitated human nature : and, in their last resort, they plead the very greatness of their own guilt, and their desert,—if they got their desert,—to be for ever cast out of God's presence. With such extraordinary arguments as these do God's saints fill their mouths when they enter in to petition and to plead before God.

Come then, and let us all join ourselves to them. Come, and let us learn to pray with them ; and, especially, to plead. And, first, let us take the case of that man here, who has been a great transgressor. Such a transgressor as he was whose great transgressions were the occasion and the opportunity of our present text. Just see what a powerful,—what an all-powerful,—argument God gives to this great transgressor in Israel to plead. Just listen to the most wonderful words. " I, even I, am He that blotteth out thy trangressions for Mine own sake, and will not remember thy sins. Put Me in remembrance : let us plead together : declare thou, that thou mayest be justified."

Let the great transgressor listen to that. Let

him lay up that in his heart. Let him plead that
with all his might, till his transgressions are all
blotted out. Let him fill his mouth with this
argument,—this unanswerable argument,—God's
own sake. Let every great transgressor, in his
great extremity, take this very text ; and, when he
has found this place, let him, on his knees, lay this
place open before God. Let him be very bold.
Let him, with all plainness, put God in remembrance
of this great promise of His. "Look down, and
see,"—let the great transgressor say with this
promise open before him and before God,—" look
down, and see if these are indeed Thine own words
to such sinners as I am. Or was the prophet
deceived in thinking that these were the very words
of the sin-pardening God ? And has he so deceived
me ? Hast Thou, O God, in very divine truth, said
that Thou wilt blot out and wilt not remember
my sins ? I shall always remember them. They
shall ever be before me. But, O my God, if ever
Thou didst blot out, and forget any man's sins,—
oh, blot out and forget mine ! " And then, from
that, still go on to plead before God the greatness
of your misery because of your sin. Tell Him that
your sin and misery are far beyond all telling.
And ask Him if it is indeed true that He " delights
in mercy." And then, plead those two great
arguments together,—your misery and His mercy.
Put Him in remembrance, that if He indeed delights

in mercy,—as He says He does,—then He will have His fill of delights in you ; for that you are of all men most miserable, and most absolutely dependent on His great mercy. And as you so pray, and so plead, ere ever you are aware, your sinful heart will break out into this song with the prophet and will say, " Who is a God like unto Thee, That pardoneth iniquity, and passeth by transgression ? Thou retainest not Thine anger for ever, because Thou delightest in mercy. He will turn again : He will have compassion upon us : Thou wilt cast all our sins into the depths of the sea."

Or, is the sanctification and true holiness of your so sinful soul,—is that your special and your always most pressing case before God ? Is it the positively awful pollution and depravity of your heart that casts you, day and night, on your face before God and man ? Is this the cry that never ceases before God from you : " Create in me a clean heart, O God " ? Is your inward enslavement to sin something you have never seen or heard equalled in Holy Scripture, or anywhere else ? Is that, indeed, so ? Then,—just say so. You cannot take into your mouth a better argument with God than that. Tell Him : put Him in remembrance : search the Scriptures : collect the promises, and plead with Him to consider your case, and to say if He has ever seen such a sad case as yours,— ever since He began to sanctify and to save sinners.

And He will surely bow down, and will hear that
cry of your heart that no mortal man hears : and
He will wipe off the tears that no mortal hand can
touch.

> When Zion's bondage God turned back,
> As men that dreamed were we :
> Then filled with laughter was our mouth
> Our tongue with melody.
> As streams of water in the south
> Our bondage, Lord, recall ;
> Who sow in tears, a reaping time
> Of joy enjoy they shall.

Or, again, are you a father, and is it your son's
bondage to sin that you are to-day pleading before
God ? If that is your case, then put Him in
remembrance that He is a Father also; and that
He has prodigal sons as well as you. And that He
has it in His power to make your heart, and your
house, as glad as His own house, and His own
heart, are again made glad, as often as any son
of His which was lost is found, and which was
dead is alive again. Read the Parable of the
Prodigal Son, and read nothing else : plead the
Parable of the Prodigal Son, and plead nothing else,
—till it is all fulfilled to you, and till you, and your
house, are all made as merry as heaven itself.

Or, is it some secret providence of God, some
secret dispensation, that is as dark as midnight to
you ? Is it some terrible crook in your lot, that
will not even out, all you can do ? Is it some cross,
so heavy that it is absolutely crushing out all faith,

and all hope, and all love, in your heart ? I have
already spoken about the Book of Job. Have you
ever read that book in real earnest ? — that so
spiritual and experimental book, written with such
a Divine intention towards such sufferers as you
are ? You must not charge God foolishly, till you
have prayed, and pled, your way through that
wonderful book. For all this time, if you only knew
it, and would but bow to believe it, God is but
putting you to school as He put His servant Job,—
if you would only read the children's school-books
and learn the children's lessons. Nay, not only so,
but God humbles Himself to plead with you about
your cross, and about your cup, since you will not
plead with Him. God puts you " in remembrance "
since you will not so put Him. " It is good,"—
so God pleads with you, and, in order to justify
Himself before you, He reasons with you and says,
" It is good for a man that he bear the yoke in his
youth. For the Lord will not cast off for ever.
But though He cause grief, yet will He have compassion according to the multitude of His mercies."
And so on, to the end of that great Divine apology
that every sufferer should have by heart. And, if
you had God's pleading with you by heart, and
always listened to it, He would surely deal with
you in your sufferings as He dealt with His own
Son in His sufferings,—He would either make your
cup to pass away from you : or else He would send

the Holy Ghost to strengthen you. Till you would boast over your very worst sufferings, and would say, "Most gladly therefore will I rather glory in my infirmities, that the power of Christ may rest upon me. For when I am weak, then am I strong."

Or, what else is your present case ? Is it old age that is fast descending on you, and that will not be rolled back ? Is it old age, age and death itself, both of which—and before very long—will claim you, and carry you off as their prey ? If that is your case—just listen to this recorded pleading of a fast-ageing saint like yourself. And make his successful pleading your own ; if, indeed, you are fast getting old, and are not entirely happy about it Plead in this way, for one hour every night : and see what your reward will be. These are that expert's very words, literally transcribed. "Having spent the day "—he said every night— "I give Thee thanks, O Lord. Evening draws nigh : make it bright. For as day has its evening, so has life : the evening of life is old age, and old age is fast overtaking me : make it bright. Cast me not off in the time of old age : forsake me not when my strength faileth me. Even to old age, be Thou He : and even to hoar hairs do Thou carry me. Abide with me, Lord, for it is toward evening, and the day of this toilful life is now far spent. The day is fled and gone : life too is fast going, this lifeless life. Night cometh : and then cometh death, the deathless death. Let the fast-coming close of my life be believing, acceptable, sinless, fearless ; and, if it please Thee, painless. And let me outstrip the night, doing, with all my might, some good work. For near is Judgment. Oh, give me a good and acceptable plea to plead in that day, O God ! " And if your heart still trembles at the thought of the cold and lonely grave, go on to plead this : " What profit is there in my blood when I go down to the pit ? Shall the dust praise Thee ? Shall it declare Thy truth ? For in death there is no remembrance of Thee : in the grave who shall give Thee thanks ? Wilt Thou shew wonders to the dead ? Shall the dead arise and praise Thee ? The living, the living, he shall praise Thee." Till, to scatter your ungodly doubts and fears, He will take pity and will Himself plead with you, and will say to you, and will put you in remembrance : " Hast thou not known ? hast thou not heard, that God giveth power to the faint ; and to them that have no might He increaseth strength ? Even the youths shall faint and be weary, and the young men shall utterly fall. But they that wait upon the Lord shall renew their strength : they shall mount up with wings as eagles ; they shall run, and not be weary ; and they shall walk, and not faint." And, as if an Old Testament prophet were not enough for your comfort, He will send you a New Testament apostle to testify and to plead with you, and to say : " For this cause we faint not : but though our outward man perish, yet the inward man is renewed day by day. While we look not at the things which are seen, but at the things which are not seen : for the things which are seen are temporal ; but the things which are not seen are eternal."

And so on, and so on. Through all your life, and in all its estates. Only, oh learn to pray, and to plead. Study to pray. Study to plead. Give yourself to prayer. Pray without ceasing. Take lessons in prayer, and in pleading. Be ambitious to become, yourselves, experts and even real authorities in prayer. It is a noble ambition. It is the noblest of all the ambitions—especially you, who are advocates and pleaders already. You have an immense start and advantage over ordinary men in this matter of prayer. And, especially, in this matter of pleading in prayer. It should be far easier for the Holy Ghost to teach our advocates to pray than to teach this heavenly art and office to any other manner of man. For every true advocate studies, down to the bottom, every case you put into his hands to plead. And much more will he study, till he has mastered, his own case before God. Every true advocate absolutely ransacks the records of the Court also for all former cases in any way similar to this case he has in hand. He puts the judge in remembrance of his own past opinions,

and of all his predecessors' past opinions and past
judgments. Not only so, but a skilful advocate will
study the very temperament and mood of mind
at the time; the age; and the very partialities and
prejudices of the judge,—so set is every adroit
advocate on carrying his case. Altogether, you
cannot but see what an advantage an advocate
has, when once he becomes a man of prayer.

But, instead of any advantage and start in
prayer, like that, you may well have this despera-
tion and hopelessness in your case, that you positively hate to pray, or even to hear about prayer.
It is not only that you have had no experience in
prayer : you would never so much as bow your
knee if it were not for one thing before you,—that
without prayer you cannot escape. Well, awful
as your case is, it is not absolutely hopeless. God
is such, and He has made such provision for you,
that even you may yet become a man of prayer;
aye, and, what is more, an advocate for other men.
Go to Him just as you are. Make your dreadful
case your great argument with Him. Say this to
Him ; say: " Lord, teach this reprobate now
before Thee to pray. Teach this castaway, if it be
possible, to pray ! Lord, soften this stone to pray !"
Tell Him the truth, and the whole truth. Tell Him,
on your knees, how you hate to come to your knees.
Tell Him that you never spent a penny upon a help
to pray. Tell Him, honestly, that, if it were not

for hell-fire, all the books and all the sermons in the world would never have brought you to His footstool. And what will He do ? Will He cast you away with contempt and indignation, as He well might, from His presence ? No ! But He will do this. He will do as all the humane crowns on earth do. When an accused man is so poor, and so friendless, that he cannot pay for a pleader, he is supplied with one of the best pleaders for nothing. And so will the Crown of heaven do with you. So God has already done with you, and for you. For, you and we,—we all,—have an Advocate with the Father. It is Christ that died ; yea, rather, that is risen again : who also maketh intercession for us. " And this Man, because He continueth ever, hath an unchangeable priesthood. Wherefore He is able to save them to the uttermost that come unto God by Him, seeing He ever liveth to make intercession for them."

> He Who, for men, their Surety stood,
> And poured on earth His precious blood,
> Pursues in heaven His mighty plan,
> The Saviour and the Friend of man.
>
> With boldness, therefore, at the throne,
> Let us make all our sorrows known;
> And ask the aids of heavenly power
> To help us in the evil hour.

XIX

CONCENTRATION IN PRAYER

" Lord, teach us to pray."—LUKE xi. 1.
" When thou hast shut thy door."—MATT. vi. 6.

WE shut our door when we wish to be alone. We shut our door when we have some special work to do that must to-day be done, some piece of work that has been far too long put off and postponed. " I must have some time to myself to-day," we say to our household. " Tell those who ask for me to-day that I am so occupied that my time is not my own. Tell them to leave their message, or to write to me. Tell them that I hope to be free, and at their service, any time to-morrow." We are deep in our accounts ; or our every thought is drunk up in some business so serious that we cannot think of anything else. We have put off and put off that imperative duty,—that so distressing entanglement,—till we can put it off not one hour longer. And then it is that we shut our door, and turn the key, and lock ourselves in and all other men and all other matters out, till this pressing matter, this importunate business, is finished and off our hands.

And then, as soon as it is finished and off our hands, we rise up and open our door. Our hands are free now. Our heart is lightened, and we are the best of company for the rest of the day.

Nothing could be plainer, and more impressive, than our Lord's words to us in the text. Just as you do every day,—He says to us,—in your household and business life, so do, exactly, in your religious life. Fix on times; set apart times. He does not say how often, or how long. He leaves all that to each man to find out for himself; only He says, When you have, and as often as you have, real business on hand with heaven; when the concerns of another life and another world are pressing you hard; when neglect and postponement will do no longer; then, set about the things of God in a serious, resolved, instant, business-like way. " Thou, when thou prayest, enter into thy closet, and when thou hast shut thy door, pray to thy Father which is in secret."

Our Lord does not mean that our Father is not in the synagogue, or even in the corners of the streets where the hypocrites of His day were wont to pray—much less that He is not present with us when our families meet together morning and evening for prayer. There is no family altar, and no prayer-meeting, and no church, and no street corner even, where God is not to be found of them that diligently seek Him. But God is present to

His children in a special and in a peculiar way when they enter their closet and shut their door. The shortest, the surest, the safest way to seek God is to seek Him " in secret." It is not that God is any more really in secret than He is in public : but we are. God is wherever we are. And God is whatever we are, in street, in synagogue, at the family altar, in the closet. It is not that God is one thing on one side of a door of wood, and another thing on the other side of that door : it is that we differ so much according to which side of that door we are on. We all feel it the instant we turn the key, and go to our knees. In that instant we are already new creatures. We feel that this is our proper, and true, and best place. We say, " This is the house of God : this is the gate of heaven." And if you keep the door shut, and give things time to work, very soon your Father and you will be the whole world to one another. And if you pursue that ; if you lay out your life to be a man of prayer ; you will make continual discoveries of practices and expedients of secret devotion, such as will carry you up to heights of heavenly-mindedness that, at one time, would have been neither believable by you, nor desirable to you. You will find out ways that will suit you, and that could not suit anyone else—ways of impressing your own heart with the Being, the Greatness, the Grandeur, the Grace, the Condescension, the Nearness, and then the Inwardness of God. Your imagination, when you are on your secret knees, will sweep through heaven and earth ; not so much seeking God as seeing Him and finding Him in all His works. You will drop down Bible history from Adam to yourself, seeing God's shining footsteps all down the way. You will see Jesus Christ also ; and will speak with Him with an intimacy and a confidence and an experience not second to the intimacy and the confidence and the experience of the disciples themselves. You will positively people your place of prayer with Jesus Christ and with His Father : and out of your place of prayer you will people your whole life, public and private, in a way, and to a degree, that would make your nearest friend to think that you had gone beside yourself, if you began to tell Him what God has done for your soul.

If we were to go over our accounts, and to arrange our disordered papers, and to write our most private letters in as short time as we give to our secret devotions, we should not need to shut our door. But our affairs are in such disorder, and in such arrears, that we must allot some time to set them right. And our Lord assumes in the text that the accounts and the correspondence connected with our religious life will need some time, and will take some trouble. We do not need to go farther than our own consciences for the proof of that. There is perhaps no man in this house who would not be put to shame if it were told what time in the day, or in the week, he gives to secret and inward prayer. Godly men go no further than their own closets for the proof of their depravity, and misery, and stupidity. Their restraint of secret prayer ; their distaste for secret prayer and a shut door ; and, with that, their treatment of their Maker, of their children, of their best friends, and of their own souls,—all horrify them when they come to themselves, and think of themselves in this matter of secret prayer.

And, even after we have taken all that to heart, and have begun to shut our door, we do not keep it long enough shut. It is quite true that secret prayer is the most purely spiritual of all human employments. That is quite true. Secret prayer is the last thing to be shut up to places, and bound down to times. At the same time we men, as Butler says, are what we are. And it is just the extreme spirituality of secret prayer that makes time, as well as seclusion, absolutely indispensable for its proper performance and for its full fruit. If we rush through a few verses of a familiar psalm, or a few petitions of the Lord's Prayer, and then up and out of our door as we should not be allowed to do in the presence-chamber of our sovereign, then we had as well,—nay, we had better,—not have gone to our knees at all. But if we enter our closet with half the fear, with half the wonder and awe,

with half the anxiety to be recognised and addressed
with which we would enter the palace of a prince
on earth, then, so willing is God to be approached
that He will immediately meet with us and will
bless us. Hurry, then, in our secret devotions, is
impossible. If you are in such a desperate hurry,
go and do the thing that so hurries you, and God
will wait. He is in no hurry. He will tarry your
leisure. No! Let there be no hurry here. God is
God; and man is man. Let all men, then, take time
and thought when they would appear before God.

And then, it sometimes takes a long time even
to get the door shut, and to get the key to turn
in the rusty lock. Last week [1] I became very
miserable as I saw my time slipping away, and my
vow not performed. I therefore one afternoon
stole into my coat and hat, and took my staff, and
slipped out of the house in secret. For two hours,
for an hour and three-quarters, I walked alone and
prayed : but pray as I would, I got not one step
nearer God all these seven or eight cold miles. My
guilty conscience mocked me to my face, and said
to me : Is it any wonder that God has cast off a
minister and a father like thee ? For two hours
I struggled on, forsaken of God, and met neither
God nor man all that chill afternoon. When, at
last, standing still, and looking at Schiehallion
clothed in white from top to bottom, this of David

[1] Preached after a holiday at Bonskeid.

shot up into my heart : " Wash me, and I shall be
whiter than snow ! " In a moment I was with
God. Or, rather, God, as I believe, was with me.
Till I walked home under the rising moon with my
head waters and with my heart in a flame of prayer ;
naming and describing, first my own children to
God, and then yours. Two hours is a long time
to steal away from one's books and companions to
swing one's walking-stick, and to utter unavailing
ejaculations to one's self in a wintry glen : but
then, my two hours look to me now—as they tasted
to me then—the best strength and the best sweetness of all my Christmas holiday.

And then, when secret, mental, and long-
accumulated intercession is once begun, it is like
the letting out of waters,—there is no end to it.
Why, my children almost made me forget you and
your children. And then, our friends ! how bad
we all are to our friends ! how short-sighted, how
cruel, how thoughtless, how inconsiderate ! We
send them gifts. Our children cover their Christmas
tree with Christmas presents to our friends. Our
friends cost us a great deal of thought and trouble
and money, from time to time. We send them
sheaves of cards with all manner of affectionate
devices and verses. We take time and we write
our old friends, at home and abroad, letters full of
news and of affection on Christmas Day and on
New Year's Day. But we never pray for them !

Or, at best, we pray for them in a moment of time, and in a great hurry. Why do we do everything for our friends but the best thing ? How few of us shut our door during all the leisure of the last fortnight, and deliberately, and particularly, and with discrimination, and with importunity prayed for our dearest and best friends ! We discriminated in our purchases for our friends, lest we should slight or offend our friends : but not in our prayers. Who in the family, who in the congregation, who in the city, who abroad, will be surprised with some blessing this year ? Surprised—with some unexpected providence, some despaired-of deliverance, some cross lifted off, or left and richly blessed, some thorn taken out of their flesh, some salvation they had not themselves had faith to ask for ? And all because we asked, and importuned, and " shut our door " upon God and ourselves in their behalf. A friend of any kind, and to any extent and degree, is something to have in this cold and lonely world. But to have a friend who has the ear of God, and who fills God's ear from time to time with our name and our case,—Oh, where shall I find such a friend ? Oh, who shall find such a friend henceforth in me ?

When a minister, going out for a long walk, takes his sick-list in his pocket ; or his visiting-book ; or his long roll of young communicants, no longer young ; or when an elder or a deacon thinks of the people of his district ; or a Sabbath school teacher

his class, and the fathers and mothers of his class ;
or a mistress her servants ; or a father his children ;
or a friend his friends ; or an enemy his enemies ;—
many a knock will come to his door before he is
done : many a mile will he have walked before he is
done. Our Lord took all night up in a mountain
over the names of His twelve disciples. And since
the day of His ascension nearly nineteen hundred
years ago He has been in continual intercession in
heaven for all those who have been in intercession
for themselves and for other men on earth. Day
and night,—He slumbers not nor sleeps : keeping
Israel by His unceasing, particular, discriminating,
importunate intercession.

Secret prayer is such an essentially spiritual duty
that the Bible nowhere lays down laws and rules
either as to times or as to places for such prayer.
The Bible treats us as men, and not as children
The Bible is at pains to tell us how this saint of God
did in his day ; and then, that other saint in his
day and in his circumstances : how Abraham did,
and Jacob, and David, and Daniel, and Jesus Christ,
and His disciples and apostles. The Bible is bold
to open the shut door of all these secret saints of
God, and to let us see them and hear them on their
knees. Abraham for Sodom : Jacob at the Jabbok :
Daniel with his open window : Jesus on the mountain all night, and in the garden at midnight : Peter
on the housetop : and Paul, in the prison and in

the workshop, for his hearers and for his readers. And then, we are left free to choose our own times and places,—few or many, open or secret, vocal or mental, just as we need, just as we like, and just as suits us.   Only,—surely nature itself, common sense itself, old habit from childhood itself, must teach and constrain us to keep our door shut for a moment or two in the morning : a moment or two alone and apart with Him Who is about our path and about our bed.   And if we once taste the strength, and the liberty, and the courage, and the light of God's countenance that always streams down on him who is found of God on his secret knees early in the morning, then that will be a sweet and a happy day that does not send us back to our knees more than once before it is over.

And then at night,—what an indecency it is, what folly !   How we shall gnash our teeth at ourselves one day to remember how a dinner-party, or music in our neighbour's house or in our own ; a friend in at supper ; a late talk ; a story-book to finish before we sleep ;—how such things as these should have been let rob us of our nightly self-examination, of nightly washing from the past day's sin, and of our nightly renewed peace with God !   What do the angels and the saints think of our folly ?   If our fathers and mothers are let look down to see what their children are doing,—would anything darken heaven to them like seeing

the things that serve their children for an excuse
to go to sleep without self-examination, confession of sin, and prayer ?   Whether they see us or
no, there is One who says over us many a graceless
and prayerless night : " Oh ! if thou hadst known !
even thou in this thy day ! "   Let us begin this
very Sabbath night.   Let us shut our door to-
night.   We are in no hurry of business or of
pleasure to-night.   Let us go back upon the morning, upon the forenoon, upon the whole day, upon
the week, upon the year.   Let us recollect for whom,
and for what, we prayed in secret this morning,—
or did not pray.   Let us recall what we read, what
we heard, and with what feelings : with whom we
conversed, and about what : all the things that
tried us, tempted us, vexed us, or helped, comforted,
and strengthened us.   Let us do that to-night,
and we shall not want matter for repentance and
prayer to-night : nor for prayer, and purpose, and
a plan of life for to-morrow.   " You are not to
content yourself," says a Queen's Physician to us
concerning the soul, " you are not to content yourself with a hasty general review of the day, but you
must enter upon it with deliberation.   Begin with
the first action of the day ; and proceed, step by
step ; and let no time, place, or action be over-
looked.   An examination," this expert says, " so
managed, will, in a little time, make you as different
from yourself as a wise man is different from an

idiot. It will give you such a newness of mind, such a spirit of wisdom, and such a desire of perfection, as you were an entire stranger to before."

" And thy Father, Which seeth in secret, shall reward thee openly." There is nothing that more humiliates us ; there is nothing that more makes us blush for shame than the way our Lord sometimes speaks about rewarding us for what we do. His words about our wages and our rewards shock us and pain us exceedingly. We know well,—we shall never forget,—that, after we have done all, we are still the most unprofitable of servants, and the most deep of debtors. At the same time,—there it stands : " Thy Father shall reward thee openly." Where ? When ? How shall He reward us openly ? Perhaps in our children,—perhaps in our children's salvation; their eternal salvation, to which they might never have attained but for our secret, unceasing, mental prayer. That would be a reward we could not refuse ! Nor feel any humiliation for, other than a most sweet and everlasting humiliation ! On the other hand, what would a kingdom be to us if anything had gone wrong with our children ? What would heaven itself be to us, if our children were not there with us ? And what a reward, what wages, if they are all there !

Or perhaps this may be it,—that when all shut doors are opened, and all secrets told out, we may be let see what we owe to one another's interces-

sions. It may be part of the first joyful surprise
of heaven to see what we did for other men and
what they did for us. " Pray for them that despitefully use you," our Lord advises us. Well, what
a surprise it will be to you and to him if some one
is brought up and introduced to you whose secret
prayers for you have been your salvation all the
time you were thinking he was your enemy, as you
were his.

But who shall tell all that is in our Lord's mind
and intention when He says : " Thy Father which
seeth in secret shall reward thee openly " ?   And
when He goes on to say, " For there is nothing
covered, that shall not be revealed : neither hid,
that shall not be known. Therefore whatsoever
ye have spoken in darkness shall be heard in the
light ; and that which ye have spoken in the ear
in closets shall be proclaimed upon the housetops."

XX

IMAGINATION IN PRAYER

" Lord, teach us to pray."—Luke xi. 1.
" Full of eyes."—Rev. iv. 8.

I NEVER see, or hear, or speak, or write the word
" imagination " without being arrested and recalled
to what Pascal and Butler and Edwards have all
said, with such power and with such passion, on the
subject of imagination. Pascal—himself all compact of imagination as he is—Pascal sets forth
again and again a tremendous indictment against
the " deceits " and " deceptions " of the imagination. Butler also, in few but always weighty words,
stigmatises the imagination as " that forward and
delusive faculty." While Jonathan Edwards, in
his own masterful way, would almost seem to have
given the death-blow to the use of the imagination
in all matters of personal and experimental religion.
But as to Butler,—that great author's latest and
best editor, in two paragraphs of really fine criticism, has clearly brought out that what Butler calls
" the errors of the imagination " are not errors of
the imagination at all, but are the errors of un-
bridled fancy and caprice, and of an unbalanced

and ill-regulated judgment. " It seems probable,"
so sums up Butler's venerable editor, " that this
is one of the rare instances in which Butler, relaxing
the firmness of his hold, forgets himself, and assumes
a licence in the use of words." And then, the editor
turns the tables on his admired author by going
on to say that, in felicity of imaginative illustration, Butler is the equal of Macaulay himself; while,
in some other of the exercises of the imagination,
Butler is even above Burke.

What, then, you will ask,—with all that,—what
exactly, and in itself, and at its best, *is* the *imagination* ? Well, come back for a moment to the very
beginning of all things, if you would have the best
answer to that question. And, then, I will answer
that question by asking and answering another
question. " How did God create man ? "—" God
created man," I am answered, " male and female,
after His own *image*, in knowledge, righteousness,
and holiness, with dominion over the creatures."
Our understanding, then, our mind and our memory,
are both so many images to us of the Divine Mind.
Our conscience, again, is an inward voice to us,
impressing upon us an imprint of the Divine
Righteousness, and the Divine Law. Our will, also,
and the Divine Will, are of the same Divine Substance. And as for our heart—it is " a copy, Lord,
of Thine." And then, in his *imagination*, man
possesses, and exercises in himself, a certain, and

that a not very far-off likeness of the Divine Omnipresence, and the Divine Omniscience. For, by his
imagination, a man can look behind, and before,
and around, and within, and above. By his imagination a man can go back to the beginning ere
ever the earth was. One man has done it. Moses
has done it. And what Moses has done to this
earth, that one day will not be remembered nor come
into mind,—all *that* John, Moses' fellow in imagination, has done to the new heaven and the new earth.
The imagination, then, whatever else it is, is not
that " forward, ever-intruding and delusive faculty " :
it is not that " author of all error," as Butler, so
unlike himself, so confuses and miscalls it. Nor is
it what Pascal so lashes to death with his splendid
invective. Nor is it imagination at all, as we have
to do with it to-day, that Edwards so denounces
in his *Religious Affections*.

Imagination, as God in His goodness gave it at
first to man,—imagination is nothing less than the
noblest intellectual attribute of the human mind.
And his imagination is far more to every spiritually-
minded man than a merely intellectual attribute
of his mind. I shall not need to go beyond Pascal
himself,—so splendidly endowed with this splendid
gift. " Imagination," says Pascal, " creates all
the beauty, and all the justice, and all the happiness
that is in the heart of man." The imagination,
then, must not be made to bear the blame that

really belongs to those men who have prostituted
it, and have filled its great inward eyes full of
visions of folly and sin : when they should have set
the Lord always before their inward eyes, with all
His works in nature, and in grace, and in glory.
Because there is only one of a city, and two of a
family, who ever employ their inward eyes aright,
—are the inward eyes of those men to be plucked
out who have on their inward eyes an unction from
the Holy One ? No. A thousand times, No !
" Open Thou mine eyes, that I may behold won-
drous things out of Thy law. I am a stranger in
the earth : hide not Thy commandments from me."

If, then, you would learn to pray to perfection,—
that is to say, to pray with all that is within you,—
never fail, never neglect, to do this. Never once
shut your bodily eyes and bow your knees to begin
to pray, without, at the same moment, opening
the eyes of your imagination. It is but a bodily
service to shut our outward eyes, and not at the
same moment open the eyes of our inner man.
Do things like this, then, when you would be in the
full spirit of prayer.   Things, more or less, like this.
" I speak as a child." Let your imagination
sweep up through the whole visible heavens, up to
the heaven of heavens. Let her sweep and soar
on her shining wing, up past sun, moon, and stars
Let her leave Orion and the Pleiades far behind
her. And let her heart swell and beat as she says

such things as these to herself: " He made all these things. *He*, Whom I now seek. That is His Sun. My Father made them all. My Mediator made them all to the glory of His Father. And He is the heir of all things. Oh, to be at peace with the Almighty! Oh, never again for one moment to forget or disobey, or displease Him! Oh, to be an heir of God, and a joint heir with Jesus Christ! Oh, to be found among the sons and the daughters of God Almighty! "

At another time, as you kneel down, flash, in a moment,—I still speak as a child,—the eyes of your heart back to Adam in his garden, and with the image of God still in all its glory upon him : and to Abraham over Sodom ; and to Moses in the cleft of the rock ; and to David in the night-watches ; and to Jesus Christ all night on the mountain top — and your time will not be lost. For, by such a flash of your imagination, at such a moment, the spirit of grace and supplications will be put in complete possession of your whole soul. Never open your eyes any morning without, that moment, seeing God and saying, " I laid me down and slept ; I awaked ; for the Lord sustained me." And never lie down without saying, " I will both lay me down in peace, and sleep : for Thou, Lord, only makest me to dwell in safety." Never set out on a journey till you have said to God and to your own soul, " The Lord shall preserve thy going

out and thy coming in from this time forth, and
even for evermore." And never so much as say
grace at table, however short time you have to say
it in, without seeing Him : in the twinkling of an
eye, be for one moment, if no more, with Him who
spreads your table, and makes your cup to run over.
In short, be sure to get a true sight and a true hold
of God, in some way or other, before you begin either
prayer or praise. There is nothing in this world so
difficult. The time it takes, sometimes, and the
toil, and the devices, and the instrumentalities—you
would not believe : because no word in all the Bible
better describes us when we are at prayer, and at
praise, and at table than this : " Without God " ; and
this: " Their hearts are far from Me." Be sure,
then—with all the help that heaven and earth,
that God and man can give you—be sure you get
your eyes and your hands on God in your prayer.
You may begin and end your prayer without that—
if you are in a hurry ; and if you have no time or
taste to give to Him Who will be honoured, and
waited on, and well pleased with you. But, if so,
you need not begin. It is not prayer at all. In
your audience of an earthly sovereign, you would
not grudge or count up the time and the pains and
the schooling beforehand. You would not begin
to speak to him while yet you were in the street,
or on the stair, and out among the common crowd.
You would keep your cause in your heart till you

were in his presence : and then, when you saw
him sitting on his throne high up above you, you
would then fall down before him, and would fill
your mouth with arguments.

Never say any of your idle words to Almighty
God. Say your idle words to your equals. Say
them to your sovereigns. But, never, as you shall
answer for it,—never, all your days,—to God. Set
the Lord always before you. Direct your prayer
to Him, and look up. Better be somewhat too
bold and somewhat unseemly than altogether to
neglect and forget Almighty God. Better say that
so bold saying,—" I will not let Thee go," than
pray with such laziness and sleepiness and stupidity
as we now pray. Look for God, and look at God :
till you can honestly say to Him, with Dr. Newman,
a great genius and a great saint, that there are now,
to you, two and two only supreme and luminously
self-evident beings in the whole universe, yourself
and your Creator. And, when once you begin to
pray in that way, you will know it. Every prayer
of yours like that will, ever after, leave its lasting
mark upon you. You will not long remain the
same man. Praying, with the imagination all
awake, and all employed—such praying will soon
drink up your whole soul into itself. You will
then " pray always." It will be to you by far the
noblest and the most blessed of all your employments in this present world. You will pray " with-

out ceasing." We shall have to drag you out of
your closet by main force. You will then be
prayerful " over much." " Whether in the body
I cannot tell ; or whether out of the body, I
cannot tell : God knoweth." Such will you all
become when you accustom your inward eyes to
see and to brood continually on the power, and on
the greatness, and on the goodness, and on the
grace and on the glory of God.

Yes, but all the time, what about this ?—you
will ask : what about this—that " no man hath
seen God at any time " ? Well,—that is true, and
well remembered, and opportunely and appropri-
ately brought forward. Whatever else is true or
false, *that* is true. That, all the time, abides the
deepest and the surest of truths. And thus it was
that the Invisible Father sent His Son to take our
" opaque and palpable " flesh, and, in it, to reveal
the Father. " And the Word was made flesh, and
dwelt among us, and we beheld His glory." And it
is this being " made flesh " of the Son of God that
has enabled us to see God. It is the birth and the
whole life, and the words, and the works, and the
death, and the resurrection, and the ascension, and
the revelation from heaven again of Jesus Christ—
it is all this that has for ever opened up such new
and boundless worlds which the Christian imagination may visit, and in which she may expatiate and
regale herself continually.

The absolute and pure Godhead is utterly and absolutely out of all reach even of the highest flights of the imagination of man. The pure and unincarnated Godhead dwells in light which no man's imagination has ever seen even afar off, or ever can see. But then, hear this. " He that hath seen Me hath seen the Father." Well, if that is true, come now ! Awake up, O my baffled and beaten-back imagination ! Awake, and look at last upon thy God ! Awake, and feast thyself for ever on thy God ! Bathe, and sun, and satiate thyself to all eternity, in the sweetness and in the beauty and in the light, and in the glory of thy God ! There is nothing, in earth or in heaven, to our imagination now like the *Word made flesh*. We cannot waste any more, so much as one beat of her wing, or one glance of her eye, or one heave of her heart on any one else, in heaven or earth, but the *Word made flesh*. " Whom have I in heaven but Thee ? And there is none upon earth that I desire beside Thee." There is a cold and heartless proverb among men to this effect : " Out of sight, out of mind." And this cold and heartless proverb would be wholly true—even of believing men—if it were not for the divine offices and the splendid services of the Christian imagination. But the truly Christian imagination never lets Jesus Christ out of her sight. And she keeps Him in her sight and ever before her inward eyes in this way. You

open your New Testament—which is her peculiar
and most delightful field,—you open that Book of
books, say, at the beginning of the Sermon on the
Mount. And, by your imagination, that moment
you are one of Christ's disciples on the spot, and are
at His feet. And all that Sermon you never once
lift your eyes off the Great Preacher. You hear
nothing else, and you see nothing else, till He shuts
the Book and says : " Great was the fall of the
house,"—and so ends His sermon. All through
His sermon you have seen the working of His face.
In every word of His sermon, you have felt the
beating of His heart. Your eye has met His eye,
again and again, till you are in chains of grace and
truth to Him ever after. And then, no sooner has
He risen up, and come down the hill, than a leper,
who dared not go up the hill, falls down at His feet,
and says, " Lord, if Thou wilt, Thou canst make
me clean ! " And all your days, ever since that
Sermon, you are that leper. All that day you have
been more and more like that leper, till now, as that
day closes, you are like him nigh unto death. You
worship Christ like the leper. He is beside you.
He stands over you. You feel, as never before,
the leprosy of sin. It fills full your polluted heart.
The diseased flesh of that poor leper is the flesh
of a little child compared with you and with your
heart. Till in a more than leper-like loathing at
yourself, and a more than leper-like despair of

yourself, you bury your face before His feet, and cry to Him : " But, Lord, if Thou only wilt, Thou canst make me clean ! "

And so on—as often as, with your imagination anointed with holy oil, you again open your New Testament. At one time, you are the publican : at another time, you are the prodigal : at another time, you are Lazarus, in his grave, beside whose dead body it was not safe or fit for a living man to come : at another time, you are Mary Magdalene : at another time, Peter in the porch : and then at another time, Judas with the money of the chief priest in his hand, and afterwards with his halter round his neck. Till your whole New Testament is all over autobiographic of you. And till you can say to Matthew, and Mark, and Luke, and to John himself : Now I believe ; and not for your sayings so much ; for I have seen Him *myself*, and have *myself* been healed of Him, and *know* that this is indeed the Christ of God, and the Saviour of the World. Never, then, I implore you, I demand of you—never, now, all the days and nights that are left to you—never open your New Testament till you have offered this prayer to God the Holy Ghost : " *Open Thou mine eyes !* " And then, as you read, stop and ponder : stop and open your eyes : stop and imagine : stop till you actually *see* Jesus Christ in the same room with you. " Lo ! I am with you alway ! " Ask Him, if He hides

Himself from you, ask Him aloud,—yes, aloud,—
whether these are, indeed, His words to you, or no.
Expect Him. Rise up, and open to Him. Salute
Him. Put down your book. Put down your light,
and then say such things as these—say : " Jesus
Christ ! Son of David ! Son of Mary ! Carpenter's Son ! Son of God ! Saviour of Sinners,
of whom I am chief ! " Speak it out. Do not be
afraid that both men and devils hear thee speaking
to thy Saviour. What about them all when thou
art alone with the Son of God ? And, besides, all
men are asleep. " Art thou, in very truth, here,
O Christ ? Dost *Thou* see *me* ? Dost *Thou* hear
me ? Yes ! Thou art *here* ! I am *sure* of it. I *feel*
it. O blessed One ! O Son of the Highest ! I am
not worthy that Thou shouldest come under my
roof. But Thou art here ! *Here,* of all the houses
in the whole city ! And, here, with *me*—O my
Saviour : *with me* of all men in the whole city ! "
Fall at His feet, kiss His feet. Kiss His feet till thy
lips come upon an iron nail in them : and, after
that, thou wilt know, of a truth, Who He is, that
is with thee in the night-watches !

But your absolutely highest, and absolutely
best, and absolutely boldest use of your imagination has yet to be told, if you are able to bear it, and
are willing to receive it. It is a very high and a very
fruitful employment of your imagination to go back
and to put yourself by means of it into the place of

Adam, and Abraham, and Moses, and Job, and Peter, and Judas, and the Magdalene, and the thief on the cross. But, to put out this magnificent talent to its very best usury, you must take the highest boldness in all the world, and put yourself in the place of CHRIST HIMSELF. Put yourself and all that is within you into the Hand of the Holy Ghost, and He will help you, most willingly and most successfully, to imagine yourself to be Jesus Christ. Imagine yourself, then, to be back in Nazareth, where He was brought up. Imagine yourself,—and show to your son and your Sunday school scholar the way to imagine himself,—sitting beside Joseph and Mary every Sabbath day in that little synagogue. Imagine yourself to be the carpenter's son, as He was. Imagine yourself at Jordan at John's great awakening of the dry bones, and then at John's Baptism. Imagine yourself fighting the devil in the wilderness with nothing but fasting and praying and the Word of God for weapons. Imagine yourself without where to lay your head. Imagine all your disciples turning against you and forsaking you. Imagine the upper room, and the garden, and the arrest and the Cross, and the darkness, and " My God, My God, why hast Thou forsaken Me ? " Did you ever imagine yourself to be crucified ? Paul did. And the imagination made him the matchless apostle of the Cross that he was. And then, imagine

yourself Christ risen, and in glory, and looking down
on *your* heart, and on *your* life, and on *your* closet,
and on *your* bed.   Imagine Him seeing *you*,—your
mind, your heart, your inspiration, your motives,
your intentions, your thoughts :—all you think,
and all you say, and all you do.   And then,—I
challenge you to imagine what HE must be thinking
and feeling, and making up His mind to-day as to
what He is to say, and to do, to you ; and when !
What would you say about yourself, if you were in His
place,—if you had died on the tree for such sins as
yours, and then saw yourself what, all this time,
you are, having no wish and no intention ever to
be otherwise ?   I think you would throw down
your office.   I feel sure you would wash your hands
of yourself.   You would say, " Let him alone ! "
You would say "Cut it down! Why cumbereth
it the ground ? "   I will tell you literally and
exactly what you would say.   From God's word
I will tell you what any honest and earnest and
wearied-out and insulted man would say, and
what may this moment, for anything you know, be
said over you from the great white throne of God.
" Because I have called, and ye refused ; I have
stretched out My hand, and no man regarded. . . .
I will laugh at your calamity ; I will mock when
your fear cometh ; when your fear cometh as desola-
tion, and your destruction cometh as a whirlwind.
. . . For that they hated knowledge, and did not

choose the fear of the Lord." Imagine the Lamb
in His wrath saying *that*! And imagine yourself
dying, and not knowing at threescore and ten how
to pray! Imagine yourself at the river, and no one
there to meet you—and no one to say to you, " I
will be with thee "! Imagine the Judge in His hot
anger saying it;—and shutting to the door—" I
never knew you "! And then, imagine with all
your might of imagination — imagine that, by an
unparalleled act of God's grace, you are sent back
again to this world, just for one more year, just
for one more week, just for one more Sabbath day
or Sabbath night! O prayer-neglecting sinner!
O equally prayer-neglecting child of God! One
more Sabbath day of the Mercy-seat, and the
Mediator at God's right hand, and the Blood of
Christ that speaketh peace!

" I have heard of Thee by the hearing of the ear:
but now, mine eye seeth Thee. Wherefore I abhor
myself, and repent in dust and ashes."

XXI

THE FORGIVING SPIRIT IN PRAYER

"Lord, teach us to pray."—LUKE xi. 1.
"When ye stand praying, forgive, if ye have ought against any."—MARK xi. 25.

PRAYER is a world by itself, a whole world, and a great world too. There is a science of prayer, and there is an art of prayer. There are more arts than one that rise out of a life of prayer, and that go to make up a life of prayer. Prayer is an education and a discipline : it is a great undertaking and a great achievement. And, like every other art, education, discipline, attainment and achievement, prayer has its own means and its own methods, its own instruments, and its own aids and appliances whereby to attain, and whereby to secure its ends.

There is a whole literature of prayer also. There are some, not small, libraries into which there is nothing else collected but the classics of prayer. There is even a bibliography of prayer. And there are bookworms who can direct you to all that has ever been written or printed about prayer ; but who never come to any eminence, or success, in prayer themselves. While, on the other hand, there are men who are recognised adepts and experts in prayer, proficient and past masters in prayer. There is nothing in which we need to take so many lessons as in prayer. There is nothing of which we are so utterly ignorant when we first begin ; there is nothing in which we are so helpless. And there is nothing else that we are so bad at all our days. We have an inborn, a constitutional, a habitual, and, indeed, an hereditary dislike of prayer, and of everything of the nature of prayer. We are not only ignorant here, and incapable : we are incorrigibly and unconquerably unwilling to learn. And when we begin to learn we need a lesson every day, almost every hour. A lesson to-day, and a lesson to-morrow ; a lesson in the morning, and a lesson at night. We need to have old lessons gone over again, revised and repeated incessantly. We need, as the schoolboys say, to go over the rudiments again and again, till we have all the axioms, and elementary rules and paradigms, and first principles of prayer made part and parcel of ourselves. Such axioms and such first principles as these : " He that cometh to God must believe that He is." " Him that cometh unto Me I will in no wise cast out." " The sacrifices of God are a broken spirit." " When ye stand praying, forgive "—these axioms and elements, and such-like.

We have had some lessons in prayer given us of late in this house ; and here is another. And,

like all our Lord's lessons, it is impossible to misunderstand it, or to forget it. No,—I must not
say that, for such is the depravity and the deceitfulness of our hearts that there is nothing that we will
not misunderstand and despise and cast behind
our back. Only, prayer—prayer sufficiently per-
severed in — will at last overmaster even our
deep depravity; and, O my brethren, what a
blessed overmastery that will be! Speak, then,
Lord! Speak once again to us what Thou wilt
have us to hear about prayer, and we will attend
this time and will obey!

1. I do not think that there is anything that our
Lord returns on so often as the forgiveness of injuries. And the reason of that may very well be
because our lives are so full of injuries, both real
and supposed, and both given and received. As
also because the thoughts and the feelings, the
words and the deeds, that injury awakens towards
one another in our hearts, are so opposed to His
mind and His spirit. It is remarkable, and we
cannot forget it, that the only petition in the
prayer that our Lord taught His disciples,—the
only petition that He repeats and underscores, as
we say,—is the fifth petition : " Forgive us our
trespasses, as we forgive those who trespass against
us." No sooner has He said *Amen* than He takes
His disciples back again to their " trespasses," and
warns them in these solemnising and arresting

words : " For, if ye forgive men their trespasses, your heavenly Father will also forgive you. But if ye forgive not men their trespasses, neither will your Father forgive your trespasses." As much as to say that the forgiveness of injuries will be the very hardest of all the holy tempers that I shall ever have to ask of you. The motions of spite and ill-will are the most difficult of all its sinful motions to subdue in the human heart. At the same time, He adds, as long as those so wicked and detestable tempers hold possession of your hearts, your prayers and everything else will be an abomination before God.

2. It is not told us in so many words, but I think I see how it came to pass that we have the text. Our Lord saw His disciples every day employing the prayer He had taught them : He heard them saying night and morning, " Forgive us our debts, as we forgive our debtors," with all their bad passions all the time in a blaze at one another. They were disputing every day who was to be the greatest. The ten " had indignation " at the two brethren because their foolish mother had asked of Christ the two chief seats in His Kingdom for her two sons. They were all trespassing every day against one another, just like ourselves, till their Master stopped them one day in the very middle of their Lord's Prayer, and said, Stand still ! stop ! say no more till you have forgiven your offending brother : and then, go on, and finish

your prayer with assurance, and with a good conscience. He laid His hand on Peter's mouth that day, and would not let Peter finish till he had, from his heart, forgiven the two ambitious brethren. And it was that arrest and interdict that his Master put upon Peter's prayer that made Peter expostulate, and say, " Lord, how oft shall my brother sin against me, and I forgive him ? " And his Master said to Peter, " I say not unto thee, Until seven times : but, Until seventy times seven." Yes, Peter, said his Master to Peter that day,—once your conscience is fully awake, and once your heart is fully broken, you will never once be able to say, Forgive me my debts, till you have already forgiven some great debtor of yours. You will always do on the spot what you ask God to do to you. And it will be by so doing that you will be a child of your Father Which is in Heaven ; Who maketh His sun to rise upon the evil and the good, and sendeth rain on the just and the unjust.

Do you ever feel that same hand stopping your mouth, my brethren ? Is *your* prayer ever cut in two and suspended, till your heart is searched out, and made quiet, and clean, and sweet to some of these, your offending brethren ? Or, better still : has Jesus Christ so penetrated and inspired your heart, and your conscience, and your imagination with His grace and His truth that you never,— either in the church or at home, either among your children or alone on your own knees,—never once say the Lord's Prayer, without naming in the middle of it, and at the fifth petition of it, some of us who vex you, or offend you, or trespass in some way against you ? some one of us towards whom you have an antipathy, or a distaste, or a secret grudge, or some inveterate ill-will ? Standing, or sitting, or kneeling, or lying on your face in prayer— is God your Witness, and your Hearer, and your Judge, that you forgive us, as often as you remember that you have ought against us ? Do you do that ? Well, I am sure if we, not to speak of God, knew that, and could believe it about you, you would not soon have occasion to forgive us again ! God bless you, all the same, and hear your prayer !

3. You would, as I think, find this to be helpful when you " stand praying," and are as yet unable to forgive. Try this the next time. Say this to yourself. Say something like this. " *What, exactly, is it that I have against that man ?* " Put it in words. Put it to yourself as you would put it to a third person. Calm reflection, and a little frank and honest self-examination, is a kind of third person, and will suffice you for his office. And so stated, so looked at, that mortal offence turns out to be not half so bad as it has up till now been felt to be. Our pride, and our self-importance, often blow up a small matter into a mortal injury. Many of our insults and injuries are far more imaginary

than real : though our sin and our misery on account of them are real enough. Look at the offender. Look closely at him. Do not avoid him. Do not refuse to have a talk with him. If possible, eat a meal now and then with him. Make a great and noble effort, and put yourself in his place in all this unhappy business. For once be honest, and just, and generous. See yourself as he has seen you. Allow and admit his side of it for a moment. Allow and admit that you differ from him, as Butler has it, quite as much as he differs from you. Let a little daylight, as Bacon has it, fall on this case that is between him and you. Let a little of the light of love, and humility, and good-will fall on him, and on yourself—and, already, your prayer is heard ! You may go on and finish your prayer now. Your trespasses are already as good as forgiven. They are : since you are all but ready to admit that a great part of your hurt and pain and anger and resentment is due to yourself, and not to your neighbour at all. And once your neighbour has come to your assistance in that way in your prayer, he will come again, and will come often, till you and he, meeting so often in amity before God, will only wait for God's promised opportunity to be the closest and the best of friends again, not only before God, but before men also. For, "He is our peace ; Who hath abolished the enmity, so making peace."

4. You will find this to be helpful also in some extreme cases. When there is some one who is trespassing against you " seven times a day "; some one whose tongue works continually against you like a sharp razor ; some one whose words are as a sword in your bones ; some one who despitefully uses you, and persecutes you ; some one who returns you only evil for all the good you have done to him and his,—and so on. There have been such extreme cases. Your own case, in short. Well. What do you wish to have done to him ? There are prayers for all kinds of cases in the Bible. And here is one for you. " Let his days be few ; and let another take his office. Let his children be fatherless, and his wife a widow. Let his children be continually vagabonds, and beg. . . . Let his posterity be cut off ; and in the generation following let their name be blotted out. . . As he loved cursing, so let it come unto him : as he delighted not in blessing, so let it be far from him." When you stand praying, put up that prayer. Say that : and then say, " For Christ's sake, Amen ! " And, then, out of the same psalm, add this for your so suffering soul : " But do Thou for me, O God the Lord, for Thy name's sake : because Thy mercy is good, deliver Thou me." I have known men to be cured of malice and ill-will by offering that prayer morning and night, and at the Lord's Table. I have known groanings, that could not be uttered

before, find utterance in the words of that devoting psalm. Try it on your enemy in the extremity of your injury and ill-will. And it will, by God's blessing, do for you and for your heart what it has done by God's blessing for far worse hearts than yours.

How horrible, and how hell-like, is a revengeful heart! While how beautiful, and how like heaven itself, is a humble, a meek, a patient, and a Christ-like heart! I have been refreshing and enlarging and ennobling my heart among Plutarch's noble Grecians and Romans in my spare hours this past winter,—when you give Plutarch in a present let it be in Thomas North's Bible English,—and at this point Plutarch's *Pericles* comes to my mind. " For he grew not only to have a great mind and an eloquent tongue, without any affectation, or gross country terms ; but to a certain modest countenance that scantly smiled : very sober in his gait : having a kind of sound in his voice that he never lost nor altered : and was of very honest behaviour : never troubled in his talk for anything that crossed him : and many such like things, as all that saw them in him, and considered him, could but wonder at him. But for proof hereof, the report goeth, there was a naughty busy fellow on a time, that a whole day together did nothing but rail upon Pericles in the market-place, and revile him to his face, with all the villainous words he could use. But Pericles put all up quietly, and gave him not a word again, dispatching in the meantime matters of importance he had in hand, till night came, that he went softly to his home, showing no alteration nor semblance of trouble at all, though this lewd varlet followed at his heels with all the villainous words he could use. But Pericles put all up quietly and gave him not a word again. And as he was at his own door, being dark night, he commanded one of his men to take a torch and take that man back to his own house." An apple of gold in a picture of silver!

But, both in patience and in forgiveness of injuries, as in all else, behold, a Greater than Pericles is here! He Who gave Pericles that noble heart is here teaching us and training us by doctrine, and by example, and by opportunity, to a nobler heart than any of Plutarch's noblest Greeks or Romans. I know nothing outside of the New Testament nobler in this noble matter than the Ethics, and the Morals, and the Parallel Lives: but I read neither in Aristotle, nor in Plato, nor in Plutarch anything like this: " Blessed are ye, when men shall revile you, and persecute you, and shall say all manner of evil against you falsely, for My sake. Rejoice and be exceeding glad: for great is your reward in heaven." Our Master, you see, actually congratulates us on our enemies, and backbiters, and false friends. He lifts us out of all our bitterness, and gloom, and despondency, and resentment, up into the sunshine of His own humble, loving, forgiving heart. And as if His heavenly teaching was not enough, He leaves us His example so that we may follow in His steps. And He leaves it—it is beautiful to see—first to Peter, who hands it down, after he is done with it, to us. Hold up, then, your hurt and proud and revengeful hearts, O all ye disciples of Christ, and let Peter, by the Holy Ghost, write this on the hard and cruel tables of your hearts. This : " Christ also suffered for us, leaving us an example, that ye should follow His steps. Who, when He was reviled, reviled not again ; when He suffered, He threatened not. . . . Who, His own self, bare our sins on His own body on the tree : . . . by whose stripes ye were healed." Come, then, my brethren, with all your wrongs and all your injuries, real and supposed, great and small ; greatly exaggerated, and impossible to be exaggerated. And when you stand praying, spread them all out before God. Name them, and describe them to Him. And He will hear you, and He will help you till you are able, under the last and the greatest of them, to say, " Father, forgive them : for they know not what they do."

XXII

THE SECRET BURDEN

" Lord, teach us to pray."—Luke xi. 1.
" Apart. . . ."—Zech. xii. 12.

> Down to Gehenna, and up to the throne,
> He travels the fastest, who travels alone.

THAT is to say, secret sin, and secret prayer, have
this in common, that they both make a man travel
his fastest. Secret sin makes him who commits
it travel his fastest down to Gehenna,—that is to
say, down into "the fire that is not quenched."
Whereas secret prayer makes him who so prays
travel his very fastest up to the throne of God, and
up to his own throne in heaven.

> Down to Gehenna, and up to the throne,
> He travels the fastest, who travels alone.

" Apart !   Apart !   Apart ! " proclaims this
prophet, ten times, in the text. If he could only
get " the house of David, and the inhabitants of
Jerusalem " to pray, and to pray *apart*—the
Fountain for sin and for uncleanness would soon
be opened ; and the Kingdom of God would soon
come. " Apart ! Apart ! Apart ! " he cries.
" Every family apart, and their wives apart ! "

This truly evangelical prophet is very importunate with the people to whom he preaches, to get
them to take the fullest and the most universal
advantage of this apartness in prayer. Apartness
in prayer has immense and incomparable advantages over all other kinds and practices of prayer :
and this prophet urges it on his people with all his
authority and with all possible earnestness. He
would have all ranks, and all classes, and all occupations, and all ages, and both sexes, to begin, and
to continue, to pray *apart*. Indeed, he as good
as proclaims to them, with all his prophetic power
and passion, that the man who does not pray apart
does not properly pray at all. And our Lord sup-
ports this prophet and says the same thing in one
of His well-known utterances about prayer. Thou,
He says, when thou prayest, go apart first. Go
away to some retreat of thine, where thou art sure
that no eye sees thee, and no ear hears thee, and
where no man so much as suspects where thou art,
and what thou art doing. Enter thy closet ; and,
with thy door shut on thee, and on thy Father
with thee,—*then pray*.

There it is—written all over our open Bible so
that he who runs may read it,—the sure and certain
blessedness of prayer *apart*, the immediate and the
immense advantage and privilege of private prayer.
But not only is all that written all over both the Old
Testament and the New, it is illustrated and en-

forced on us out of our own experience every day. Let us just take ourselves here as so many proofs and pictures of the advantage and superiority and privilege of *private prayer* over *public prayer*. And take just your minister and then yourselves in proof and in illustration of this. As soon as the church bells stop ringing on the Sabbath morning, your ministers must immediately begin to pray openly and before men—whether they are prepared or no ; whether they are in the proper spirit or no ; and whether they have recovered their lost sight and lost hold of God that morning or no. It is expected of them that, as soon as the opening psalm is sung, the pulpit should begin to pray.

And you get,—more or less,—every Sabbath morning from the pulpit what you pay your seat for, and demand of us in return. You get a few well-repeated liturgical passages. You get a few well-selected texts taken out of the Psalms. And then a promise or two taken out of the prophets and the apostles,—all artistically wound up with a few words of doxology. But all that, four or five times every Sabbath day, is not prayer. All that is a certain open and public acknowledgment and tribute to the House of Prayer, and to the Day of Prayer ; but nobody with an atom of sense or spirit ever supposes that *that* is prayer. And then we have to stop our Sabbath morning prayer before we have well begun it. You allow, and measure

out to us by your watches, our limit. We must say
our pulpit prayers before you at the proper moment,
in the proper tones, and to the proper length,—on
the pain of losing your countenance and patronage.
And on the other hand, though our hearts are
breaking, we must begin at the advertised hour.
And we must not by a sigh, or a sob, or a tear, or by
one utterance of reality and sincerity, annoy or
startle or upset you. We must please you with
a pleasant voice. Our very pronunciation and
accent must be the same as yours,—else you will
not have it. We may let out our passions in everything else, as much as we like,—but not on Sabbath,
and, above all, not in pulpit prayer. These are
some of the inconveniences and disadvantages and
dangers of public prayer to your ministers. But
out of the pulpit, and sufficiently away and apart
from you,—we can do what we like. We have no
longer to please you to your edification. We can
wait as long as we like in our closet, before we
attempt to pray. The day is over now, and the
duties of the day : we are in no hurry now : we
are under no rule of use and wont now. We can
watch a whole hour now, if we are not too tired and
sleepy. We can sit down and read, and muse, and
meditate, and make images of things to ourselves
out of our Bible, or out of our Andrewes, till the fire
begins to burn ! That was what David did. " My
heart was hot within me, while I was musing the fire

burned: then spake I with my tongue." And the minutes toward midnight may run on to hours ; and the midnight hours to morning watches ; and yet we will run no danger of wearying out Him who slumbers not nor sleeps : He still waits to be gracious. What we ministers, of all men, would do without prayer apart,—I cannot imagine what would become of us ! But, with his closet, and with the key of his closet continually in his hand, no minister need despair, even though he is a great orator, with a great gift of public prayer. " Apart ! Apart ! Apart ! " this great prophet keeps ringing in every minister's ears. " Apart ! Apart ! Apart ! Every minister—of all men,—apart ! "

And the very same thing holds true of yourselves, my praying brethren. You have the very same out-gate and retreat in private prayer that we have. You can escape apart from us, and from all our pulpit prayers. God help you if you do not ! If all your praying is performed here,—and if it is all performed by your minister for you,—may God pity you, and teach you Himself to pray ! But if you are living a life of secret prayer, *then* you are not dependent on us ; and we are not so ruinously responsible for you. And indeed, if you pray much apart, you are already beyond our depth. You are wiser than all your teachers. You could teach us. I sometimes see you, and see what you are thinking about, when you are not aware. You listen to us in our public prayers. And you smile to yourself as you see us attempting a thing in public that—you see quite well—we know next to nothing about in private. We have our reward of others, but not of you : you say nothing. You sit out the public worship, and then you rise up, and go home. It is with you as when a hungry man dreameth and ; behold, he eateth ; but he awaketh and his soul is empty. Till you get home, and the house is asleep. And then, could we but act the eaves-dropper that night ! Could we but get our ear close to your keyhole, we should learn a lesson in prayer that we should not forget. You must surely see what I am driving at in all this, do you not ? I am labouring, and risking something, to prove this to you, and to print it on your hearts,—the immense privilege and the immense and incom-parable opportunity and advantage of *private* prayer, of prayer apart.

And then, for a further illustration of this argu-ment, take the *confession of sin*, in public and in private prayer. The feeling of sin is the most personal, and poignant, and overpowering part of your daily and hourly prayer. And, if you will think about it for one moment, you will see how absolutely impossible it is for you to discover, and to lay bare and to put the proper words and feelings upon yourself and upon your sin, in *public* prayer You cannot do it. You dare not do it. And when you do do it, under some unbearable load of guilt, or under some overpowering pain of heart,—you do yourself no good, and you do all who hear you real evil. You offend them. You tempt them to think and to speak about you and your prayers, which is a most mischievous thing: you terrify, like Thomas Boston, the godly. And, after all; after all that injurious truthfulness and plain-spokenness of yours in prayer,—with all that, you cannot in public prayer go out sufficiently into particulars and instances, and times, and places, and people. *Particularity*, and *taking instances*, is the very life-blood of all true and prevailing prayer. But you dare not do that: you dare not take an outstanding instance of your daily sinfulness and utter corruption of heart in public or in family prayer. It would be insufferable and unpardonable. It is never done. And you must not under any temptation of conscience, or of heart, ever do it. When your door is shut, and when all public propriety, and all formality, and insincerity is shut out, *then* you can say and do anything to which the spirit moves you. You can pray all night on your face, if you like, like your Lord in Gethsemane. When you are so full of sin that you are beside yourself with the leprosy of it and with the shame and the pain of it,—they would carry you to the madhouse, if you let yourself say and do in public what all God's greatest saints, beginning with God's Son, have continually done in

private. But your soul may sweat great drops of
blood in secret, and no human being is any wiser.
And as for those who watch you and see it all,—
" there is joy in heaven " over you from that night.
Not one in ten of you have ever done it, possibly
not one in a hundred : but when you begin really
to look on Him whom you have pierced, as this
great prophet has it, then you will begin to understand what it is to be in bitterness, and to mourn
apart, as one is in bitterness for his first-born.
Then, no pulpit confession, and no family altar, will
relieve your heart. For then, there will be a life-
long mourning in your heart as the mourning of
Hadadrimmon in the valley of Megiddon. " Oh,"
you will cry, " oh, that mine head were waters, and
mine eyes a fountain of tears, that I might weep
day and night for the Son of God whom I have
slain by my sin! Oh, that I had in the wilderness
a lodging-place of wayfaring men ; that I might
leave my people, and go from them to weep for my
sin against my God and my Saviour ! " And God
will provide such a place *apart* for you, and for
Himself with you,—till one day, when your head
is, as never before, " waters," He will say : " It is
enough, go in peace. Weep no more." And He
will wipe all tears from your eyes.

And the very same thing holds true of all *intercessory* prayer. It would be an impertinence and
an impudence ; it would be an ostentation and a

presumption to pray for other men in public, as you are permitted and enabled and commanded to pray for them in private. It would be resented, and never forgiven. In intercessory prayer in public, particulars and instances, and actual persons, and special and peculiar cases, are absolutely impracticable and impossible. You simply dare not pray, in public, for other men,—any more than for yourself,—as they need to be prayed for. You would be arrested and imprisoned under the law of libel if you did it. Were you to see these men and women around you as they are ; and were you to describe them, and to plead with God to redeem and renew, and restore, and save them,— the judge would shut your mouth. But in private, neither your friend nor your enemy will ever know, or even guess, till the last day, what they owe to you, and to your closet. You will never incur either blame or resentment or retaliation by the way you speak about them and their needs in the ear of God. The things that are notoriously and irrecoverably destroying the character and the usefulness of your fellow-worshipper—you may not so much as whisper them to your best friend, or to his. But you can, and you must, bear him by name, and all his sins and vices, all that is déplorable, and all that is contemptible about him, before God. And if you do so ; and if you persist and persevere in doing so,—though you would not believe it,—you will come out of your closet to love, and to honour, and to put up with, and to protect, and to defend your client the more,—the more you see what is wrong with him, and the more you importune God in his behalf. Intercessory prayer, in the pulpit, usually begins with the Sovereign, and the Royal Family, and the Prime Minister, and the Parliament, and so on. You all know the monotonous and meaningless rubric. But nobody is any better, Sovereign nor Parliament, because nobody is in earnest. We pray for the Sovereign, in order to be seen and heard and approved of men. But in secret,—it is another matter. If you ever—before God and in faith and love—prayed for your Sovereign, or for any great personage sincerely, and with importunity, you then began to feel toward them in a new way ; and you began to have your answer returned into your own bosom, if not yet into theirs, in the shape of real honour, and real love, and real good-will, and real good wishes, and more and better prayer, for those you so pray for. " I exhort therefore that, first of all, supplications, prayers, intercessions, be made for all men; for kings, and for all that are in authority ; that we may lead a quiet and peaceable life in all godliness and honesty. . . . For there is one God, and one Mediator between God and men, the Man Christ Jesus. . . . I will therefore that men pray everywhere, lifting up holy hands, without wrath and doubting."

And, then,—to conclude this great argument,— take *thanksgiving*, which is, by far, the best and the most blessed part of both public and private prayer. You cannot thank God with all your heart in public. You cannot tell in public—even to them that fear God—all that God has done for your soul. Even David himself could not do it. He tried it, again and again : but he had to give up the attempt. In public, that is, and before the great congregation, he could not do it. You see him attempting it, again and again ; but the great congregation is not able to bear it. Here is the best specimen of a true thanksgiving I have ever met with. But then, it is not a public, but a private devotion,—as its title-page bears.

" O God," this man of prayer said in secret to God once every week, taking a whole night to it : going out into particulars, and giving instances, and names, and dates.

" O God, I thank Thee for my existence : for my life, and for my reason. For all Thy gifts to me of grace, nature, fortune "—(enumerating and naming them, and taking time to do it)—" for all Thy forbearance, long-suffering, long long-suffering to me-ward, up to this night. For all good things I have received of Thy hand "—(naming some of them)—" for my parents honest and good " (re-collecting them, and recollecting instances and occasions of their honesty and goodness)—" and

for benefactors, never to be forgotten" (naming
them). "For religious, and literary, and social
intimates, so congenial, and so helpful. For all
who have helped me by their writings,—(and at
that he rises off his knees, and walks round his
library, and passes his eye along its so helpful
shelves).—"For all who have saved my soul also
by their sermons, and their prayers" (and at this
he recalls great preachers of the soul, some dead,
and some still alive and open to his acknowledg-
ments). "For all whose rebukes and remon-
strances have arrested and reformed me. For
those even who have, some intentionally, and
some unintentionally, insulted and injured me,—
but I have got good out of it all,"—and so on.
You could not offer a sacrifice of praise like that
before everybody. You could not do it with
propriety before anybody! And it would be still
more impossible to go on, and to give instances
and particulars like this : and, without instances
and particulars, you might as well be in your bed.
"Thou holdest my soul in life, and sufferest not my
feet to be moved. Thou rescuest me every day
from dangers, and from sicknesses of body and soul ;
from public shame, and from the strife of tongues.
Thou continuest to work in me, by Thy special
grace to me, some timeous remembrance of my
latter end ; and some true recollection and shame,
and horror, and grief of heart for my past sins.

Glory be to thee, O God, for Thine unspeakable, and unimaginable goodness to me,—of all sinners the most unworthy, the most provoking, and the most unthankful!" You could not say things like that in the pulpit, no, nor at your own most intimate family altar. And, yet, they *must* be said. There are men among you whose hearts would absolutely burst, if they were not let say such things : aye, and say them, not once a week, like this great saint, but every day and every night. And it is to them—few, or many among us, God alone knows,—it is to *them* that this Scripture is selected and sent this morning,—this Scripture : And I will pour out upon them the spirit of grace and of supplications, the spirit of repentance and confession, the spirit of intercession and prayer for all men : and the still more blessed spirit of praise and thankfulness : and they shall pray and praise *apart*, till their Father which seeth, and heareth, apart and in secret, shall reward them openly.

> Down to Gehenna, and up to the throne,
> He travels the fastest, who travels alone,

XXIII

THE ENDLESS QUEST

" Lord, teach us to pray."—LUKE xi. 1.
" He that cometh to God must believe that He is, and that He
is a rewarder of them that diligently seek Him (lit. that seek
Him out)."—HEB. xi. 6.

I MUST not set myself up as a man able to mend,
and to make improvements upon, the English
translation of the Greek Testament. At the same
time, it seems to me to be beyond dispute that the
English of the text falls far short of the exact point
and the full expressiveness of the original. *Rem
acu :*—touching the text with the point of a needle,
Bengel exclaims : " A grand compound!" And it
is a " grand compound." The verb in the text
is not simply *to seek*. It is not simply to seek diligently. It is *to seek out* : it is to seek and search
out to the very end. A Greek particle, of the
greatest possible emphasis and expressiveness, is
prefixed to the simple verb : and those two letters
are letters of such strength and intensity that they
make the commonplace word to which they are
prefixed to shine out with a great grandeur to
Bengel's so keen, so scholarly, and so spiritual eyes.

Ever feeling after God, if haply I may find Him, in a moment I saw the working out of my own salvation in a new light ; and, at the same moment, I saw written out before me my present sermon, as soon as I stumbled on the Apostle's "grand compound." " But without faith it is impossible to please Him : for he that cometh to God must believe that He is, and that He is a rewarder of them that seek Him out " to the end; of them that seek Him out saying, " Oh, that I knew where I might find Him ! " That seek Him out saying, " Verily, Thou art a God that hidest Thyself." That seek Him out with their whole heart. That seek Him with originality, with invention, with initiation, with enterprise, with boldness, with all possible urgency, and with all possible intensity and strenuousness. As also, to the end of a whole life of the strictest obedience, and the most absolute and unshaken faith, and hope, and love. " A grand compound ! "

As we go on in life, as we more and more come to be men and leave off speaking as children, and understanding as children and thinking as children, we come to see with more and more clearness what it is to us,—what it must be to us,—to arise and return to God, to seek God, to come to God, and to walk with God. At one time we had the most unworthy and impossible thoughts of God, and of our seeking Him, and finding Him. We had the most

materialistic, and limited, and local, and external
ideas about God. But, as we became men, we
were led,—all too slowly, and all too unwillingly,—
yet we were led to see that God is an Infinite and
an Omnipresent Spirit : and that they that would
seek God must seek Him in the *spiritual world*,
that is, in that great spiritual world of things into
which out own hearts within us are the true, and
the only, door. " Thou hast set the world in their
hearts," says the Preacher in a very profound
passage. The spiritual world, that is ; the world
of God, and of all who are seeking God out till they
are rewarded of Him. " We do not come to God
upon our feet," says Augustine, " but upon our
affections." And thus it is that we, who are so
materialistically minded and so unspiritually minded
men, find it so distasteful, and so difficult, and so
impossible to seek out God till we find Him.
Were He to be found in any temple made with
hands ; were He to be found in Samaria or in
Jerusalem, between the Cherubim on earth, or on a
throne in heaven,—then, we should soon find Him.
But because He has set the spiritual world, and
Himself as the God and King of the spiritual world,
in our own hearts,—we both mistake the only way
to find Him, and miss our promised reward of Him.

How can I go away from Him,—and how can I
come back to Him, Who is *everywhere present* ?
" Whither shall I go from Thy spirit ? or whither

shall I flee from Thy presence ? If I ascend up
into heaven, Thou art there. If I make my bed
in hell, behold, Thou art there." A question, a
chain of questions like that, put continually, put
imaginatively, put day and night and in dead
earnest to a man's self, will be the beginning of a
new life to any man among us. Questions, prob-
lems, psalms and prayers, like that,—raised, reasoned
out, understood, and accepted,—will open our eyes.
A man has no sooner stated these things to himself
than, from that moment, he begins to see as never
before, something of the greatness and the glory
of God ; something of the Divine and Holy Spirituality of God ; and, consequently, something of the
pure spirituality of all his intercourse with God.
I see then, that it is not God who has turned away
and removed Himself from me in His omnipresence
and omniscience : but that I have gone away and
removed myself far from Him in all my thoughts
and words and deeds. I have gone away from
God *in my heart*. And, as my going away from
God was, so must my coming back to Him be.
And thus we are told of the prodigal son that his
coming to himself was his first step back to his
father. And his whole return began, and was
carried out, by recollection, and by repentance,
and by confidence in his father's forgiveness, and
by a resolution, at once acted on, to return to his
father's house. The whole parable took place in

his own heart. The far country was all in that
prodigal son's own heart. The mighty famine was
all in his own heart. The swine and their husks
were all in his own heart. The best robe and the
ring and the shoes were all in his own heart. And
the mirth and the music and the dancing were all
also in his own heart. " He hath set the whole
world," says the wise man, " in their heart."

Take then, as the first illustration of this law of
our text, take the truly studious, or, as I shall call
him, the truly philosophic seeker after *truth*, if not
yet to say after GOD. Let that student be, at
present, a total stranger to God. Nay, I am bold
to say, let him be at secret enmity with God. Only,
let him be an honest, earnest, hard-working, still-
persevering, and everyway-genuine student of
nature and of man. Let him never be content
with what he has as yet attained, but let him love,
and follow, and seek out, the whole truth to the
end. Now such a true student as that will not
work at his studies with one part of his mind only;
but in the measure of his depth, and strength, and
wisdom, he will bring all that is within him, as the
Psalmist says, to his studies. He will bring his
heart as well as his head : his imagination as well
as his understanding : his conscience even, and his
will, as well as his powers of recollection and reasoning. And as he works on, all the seriousness, all
the reverence, all the humility, all the patience and

all the love with which he studies nature, will more
and more be drawn out as he ponders and asks,—
who, or what, is the real root, and source, and great
original of nature and man ? Who made all these
things ? And for why ? And by this time, that
true student has come, all unawares to himself,
under the sure operation of that great Divine law,
which is enunciated with such certitude in this
splendid text. For he that cometh seeking God,
whether in nature or in grace ; whether in God's
works, or in God's Son, or in God's word : if he
still comes with teachableness, and with patience,
and with humility, and with faith, and with hope,
and with love to the end,—all of which are the
qualities and the characters of a true student,—
that man, by this time, is not far from God. Till
the very vastness, and order, and beauty, and law-
abidingness, and loyalty, and serviceableness of
nature, will all more and more pierce his conscience,
and more and more move, and humble, and break
his heart. And God will, to a certainty, reward
that man, that serious, and honest, and humble-
minded man, by putting this psalm in his mouth,
till he will join his fellow-worshippers here in singing
it : " The heavens declare the glory of God, and
the firmament sheweth His handywork." But it
is the law of the Lord that is perfect, converting
the soul : it is the testimony of the Lord that is pure,
enlightening the eyes. " It is true that a little

philosophy inclineth man's mind to atheism :
but depth in philosophy bringeth men's minds
about to religion : for while the mind of man looketh
upon second causes scattered, it may sometimes
rest in them, and go no further : but when it be-
holdeth the chain of them confederate and linked
together, it must needs fly to Providence and Deity.
Then, according to the allegory of the poets, he
will easily believe that the highest link of nature's
chain must needs be tied to the foot of Jupiter's
chair."

We speak in that large and general way about
what we call great students and great thinkers
and great philosophers, as they feel after, and find
out God ; and we do not speak amiss or out of place.
But there is no student in all the world like the
student of his own heart.   There is no thinker so
deep and difficult as he who thinks about himself.
And out of all the philosophies that have been from
the beginning, there is none of them all like that of
a personal, a practical, an experimental religion,
and an out-and-out obedience to all God's commandments.   That is science.   That is philosophy.
As the Book of Revelation has it : " Here is wisdom " :
and " Here is the mind which hath wisdom."   The
mind, that is, which seeks God in all things, and at all
times, and that seeks Him out till it finds Him.   And
till God says to that man also, " Fear not, Abram :
I am thy shield and thy exceeding great reward."

Is there any man here then, this day, who is
saying : " Oh, that I knew where I might find Him !
That I might come even to His seat " ?   What is
the matter with you, man ?   What is it that has so
banished your soul away from God ?   What was
it that so carried you away into that captivity ?
And what is the name of the chain that holds you
so fast there ?   Do you ask honestly and in earnest,
—" What must I do to be saved from this far
country, this hell-upon-earth into which I have
fallen ? "   O man !   *You* are very easily answered.
Your case is very easily treated.   You are not a great
thinker : you are simply a great sinner.   It is not
speculation that has led you astray, but disobedience, and a bad heart.   You must not expect to be
flattered and fondled, and sympathised and con-
doled with, as if there was some deep and awful
mystery about you.   Oh no !   there is nothing
mysterious or awful about you.   You are a quite
commonplace, everyday, vulgar transgressor.   There
are plenty like you.   " Say not in thine heart,
Who shall ascend into heaven ? . . . Or, Who shall
descend into the deep ? . . . But what saith it ?
The word is nigh thee."   That is the word of repentance, and return to God, and a better life, and a
broken heart, which we preach to ourselves and
to you.   Do you not understand ?   Do you not
know what it is in you, and about you, that lands
you in such nakedness and famine and shame and

pain and death ? You know quite well. It is *sin*.
It is nothing but sin. It is the sins and the faults
of your heart and your life. Now, *this* is wisdom.
This is the mind that hath wisdom. To put your
finger on yourself and say : It is in *this*, and in *this*,
and in *this*, that I always go away from God.
It is in the indulgence of this appetite. It is in
this wicked temper. It is in this secret envy and
ill-will. It is in this sour and sullen heart. It is in
this secret but deep dislike and evil mind at that
man who so innocently trusts me, and who so
unsuspiciously thinks me his friend. It is in this
scandalous neglect of prayer ; this shameful, this
suicidal neglect of all kinds of personal religion
in the sight of God. Believe the worst about yourself. Fix on the constantly sinful state of your own
heart, and on the secret springs of sinful thought
and feeling within you : *seek yourself out*, as the
text says, and you are thus seeking out God. And
the more evil you seek out of yourself,—and put it
away,—the nearer and the surer you will come to
God. Fight every day against no one else but
yourself ; and against nothing else but every
secret motion of pride, and anger, and malice, and
love of evil, and dislike of good. Every blow you deal
to these deadly things of which your heart is full
is another safe and sure step back to God. At
every such stroke at yourself, and at your own sin,
God will by all that come back to you ; till, at last,

He will fill your whole soul with Himself. That was
the way, and it was in no other way, that Enoch
" walked with God " in the verse just before the text.
And you too will walk with God, and God with you,
just in the measure in which you put on humility,
and put off pride; and fill your hot heart full of the
meekness and lowly-mindedness of the Son of God ;
and, beside it, with the contrition, and the penitence,
and the watchfulness, and the constant prayerful-
ness of one of His true disciples. To hold your
peace when you are reproved,—that is a sure step
toward God. To let a slight, a contempt, an affront,
an insult, a scoff, a sneer, fall on your head like an
excellent oil, and on your heart like your true desert
—" with that man will I dwell," says the God of Israel
and the God and Father of our Lord Jesus Christ.
Every step you take out of an angry and wrathful
heart, and out of a sour, sullen, and morose heart,
and into a meek and peace-making heart, out of
envy and uneasiness, and into admiration and
honour; on the spot your heavenly Father will
acknowledge and will reward you. *Seek Him out* :
and see if He will not !

And, then,—remaining always at your true post,
within yourself,—come out continually in that mind,
and seek out God in *all outward things also*. For, be
sure, He is in all outward things as well : and He
is in them all for you to seek Him out till you are
rewarded of Him. In every ordinance of His grace

and truth He is to be sought out by you. On every new Sabbath, and in every psalm, and prayer, and scripture, and silent and secret hour of that Sabbath. In every week-day providence also. He is in every providence of His for many more beside you : but He is there for you, just as much as if He were there for no one but you. In public providences, in domestic providences, as well as in all those more secret and personal providences that have been so many perfect miracles in your life. And in every change and alteration in your circumstances. God, all-wise, does not make a change in your circumstances just for the love of change. It is all for His love to you, and to make you seek out a fresh proof of that love, as well as to draw out some new, and warm, and wondering love out of your renewed heart to Him. After you have appropriated to yourself all the reward He had prepared for you in one age and stage of your life, He leads you on to another age and another stage : and He hides Himself and His grace there for you again to seek Him out. And this goes on, all through your life, till He teaches you to say, " One thing do I desire, and that will I seek after, and that is God, my God, my Life, my Joy, my Blessedness."

Men and women ! What are you living for ? What is your life yielding you ? If you are not finding God in all parts of your life—what a fatal mistake you are making ! And what a magnificent reward you are for ever missing !

But, when all is said, it is not to be wondered at that so few of us seek, and *seek out*, God. For His greatness passes all comprehension, and imagination, and searching out, of men and angels. His holiness also makes Him a " consuming fire " to such sinners as we are. And then, His awful spirituality, omnipresence, and inwardness,—we would go mad, if we once saw Him as He is, and at the same time saw ourselves as we are. " And He said, There shall no man see Me, and live." We must grow like God before we can both see Him and live. And thus it is that it is only His very choicest and chiefest saints who do seek Him out to the end either in His Son, or in the Scriptures, or in their own hearts, or in Providence, or in nature, or in unceasing prayer. It is only one here, and another there, who ever get the length of crying out with Job, " Oh, that I knew where I might find Him." And with Isaiah, " Verily Thou art a God that hidest Thyself." And with Paul, " Dwelling in light which no man can approach unto : Whom no man hath seen, or can see."

But, just in the depth and adoration of their cry ; and just as their sight and sense is of the greatness and the glory of God,—just in that kind, and just in that degree, will their reward be, when He shall reveal Himself at last, and shall Himself

become their exceeding great and everlasting Reward
And though we are not worthy to stoop down and
unloose the latchet of the shoes of such great, and
such greatly rewarded, saints of God : yet, if we
also seek God, and seek Him out to the end of our
life,—feeble as our faith is, and smoking flax as
our love is,—yet by His grace, after all our partial
discoveries of God, and all our occasional experiences of Him, we also in our measure shall receive,
and shall for ever possess, and enjoy very God
Almighty Himself for our own Reward for ever.

" Oh, the depth of the riches both of the wisdom
and the knowledge of God ! . . . For of Him, and
through Him, and to Him, are all things." " Whom
have I in heaven but Thee ? And there is none
upon earth that I desire beside Thee." " My soul
longeth, yea, even fainteth : . . . my heart and
my flesh cry out for the living God. . . . They go
from strength to strength, every one of them in
Zion appeareth before God."